CHRI
ROYAL

BRIAN JONES

REVIEW AND HERALD® PUBLISHING ASSOCIATION
HAGERSTOWN, MD 21740

Texts credited to ASV are from *The Holy Bible*, edited by the American Revision Committee, Standard Edition, Thomas Nelson & Sons, 1901.

Texts credited to NIV are from the *Holy Bible, New International Version*. Copyright © 1973, 1978, 1984, International Bible Society. Used by permission of Zondervan Bible Publishers.

Texts credited to NKJV are from The New King James Version. Copyright © 1979, 1980, 1982, Thomas Nelson, Inc., Publishers.

Bible texts credited to RSV are from the Revised Standard Version of the Bible, copyright © 1946, 1952, 1971, by the Division of Christian Education of the National Council of the Churches of Christ in the U.S.A. Used by permission.

Bible texts credited to TEV are from the *Good News Bible*—Old Testament: Copyright © American Bible Society 1976; New Testament: Copyright © American Bible Society 1966, 1971, 1976.

Texts credited to Weymouth are from Richard Francis Weymouth, *The New Testament in Modern Speech* (London: James Clarke & Co., 1903).

This book was
Edited by Richard W. Coffen
Cover photo by Photo Disc
Cover illustration by Russ Harlan
Cover design by Helcio Deslandes
Typeset:11/12 Times

PRINTED IN U.S.A.

99 98 97 96   5 4 3 2 1

R&H Cataloging Service
Jones, Brian
    Christ's royal bride.

    1. Church.   I. Title.

            262.7

ISBN 0-8280-1053-6

Contents

The King's Consort

Rising above the ruins of human pride

Stands the church, in bright robes of majestic weave

Fashioned by the hands of her Lord crucified.

She stands, not statue-like as some beguiled Eve,

But as the handmaid of her King, single-eyed

To His glory through the stormy eventide;

Alert to His pleading voice that cries reprieve

For a world rushing to its ruinous end,

And bids His handmaid go more than to relieve

Mortal wounds of stricken souls, but to extend

His life-touch and word to all who will believe

And receive her Lord as *their* Saviour and Friend.

Though scourged by some, to shame she is crucified;

For this travailing maid is Christ's royal bride.

Introduction

Church. Is it a luxury for Christians with plenty of spare time, an optional blessing to be taken or left as suits our inclination and convenience? Is it a political organization for religious hacks bent on maintaining their positions and power? Is it a haven for hypocrites who, by their show of piety, hope to deceive God into thinking that they are fit for heaven? Or is it something honorable, enduring, and good?

Scripture declares that the church is the "pillar and ground of the truth" (1 Tim. 3:15). An anointed writer says that it is "the case which contains His jewels, the fold which encloses His flock" *(Testimonies,* vol. 6, p. 261), "the court of holy life" *(Our High Calling,* p. 164).

Yet the church is composed of undeniably fallible persons. Pastors who stumble, laity who flounder, at least some of the time. But the church consists of more than people; it also includes Christ, who is the head of the church, while its members constitute His body (Eph. 1:22, 23). Christ's headship over the church establishes its value, permanence, and legitimate authority. Without Him the church would be nothing more than an aggregate of religious people, an ecclesiastical club.

It is very much in vogue to be cynical about "church." Crooked pastors, garish worship services, popular "feel good" psychology in the pulpit, eerie cultic practices, religious coalitions with an ominous political agenda, interdenominational rivalry, and religious wars all combine in a nauseating mélange to make the whole concept of the church seem repulsive, even dangerous, to many people, both religious and nonreligious. But these are anomalies.

The church, as conceived by Christ, had no such marred features. He created the church to be His holy bride through which the glory of His own character would be reflected without distortion or dissimulation (Eph. 5:25-32). He created the church to be His ministering hands and beckoning voice to reach the world with the saving power of His gospel. He created the church to be His bosom of comfort to a spiritually derelict world that lives in agonizing alienation from its loving God.

Christ has provided for His church to achieve a glorious completion of all His purposes for it. Satan has often besmeared the church with His disguising cosmetics and clothed it in harlot's attire, but it shall yet emerge, through the wonder-working power of Christ, "a glorious church, not having spot, or wrinkle, or any such thing; but . . . holy and without blemish" (verse 27).

This book traces God's plan in making the church "His fortress in a revolted world" *(Signs of the Times*, Mar. 3, 1898) and His holy bride—such a fortress as the gates of hell shall not prevail against, and such a bride as no tempter can defile or seduce.

Like the
Stars Forever

1

Douglas didn't go to church. Transcendentalist, recluse, pacifist, reveler was he, but definitely not a churchgoer. He prided himself on being a nonjoiner, aligned with no party, persuasion, or program. Free among the dropouts, psychedelic explorer, cosmic frontiersman blazing new trails to Nirvana—that was Douglas. To him the idea of going to church was stuffy, shallow, and dull—a dreary tradition of mindless conformists too scared or unimaginative to face the liberating reality that all people are naturally divine with or without religion. Through his late teens and early 20s Douglas blithely sailed through life, delighting in the unconventionality of his views.

A dropout at 18, Douglas lived in a rude hut deep in the woods along California's northern coast. Jazz, mystical books, wine, and hallucinogenic drugs were his all-absorbing pursuits. With little money, no job, no commitments, no plans or recognized responsibilities of any kind, Douglas's days drifted aimlessly away.

But then his teeth began to hurt. Several years of negligent hygiene and defective diet brought acute dental problems when he was 23. Driven from his cherished solitude by pain, he made his way to the nearest dental office, 20 miles from his woodland lair. Although penniless, Douglas hoped to gain the compassion of the dentist. And he did, because this dentist and his wife, who assisted him, were true Christians.

Through his contact with Dr. Frank and Evelyn Earl, Douglas was drawn to Christ. And even though he had always regarded the

Bible as a book of silly myths, shackling rules, and deceptive notions, Douglas started reading the Bible to see what ideas it attributed to Jesus of Nazareth and what biographical tidbits it might contain on the life of this founder of Christianity. After all, he'd met two of Jesus' admirers who were kind, generous, and intelligent. They certainly seemed sincere and committed to their beliefs in a practical way. They not only gave him much free dental care, but also invited him to their home. On one occasion they gave him a large sack of oranges to help him recover from a cold. Never did they ask anything in return for their kindness or give the impression that they desired any reciprocation.

As Douglas continued studying his Bible, he came to know Christ personally as his own Saviour. He was freed from his addiction to tobacco, alcohol, marijuana, and the whole array of psychedelic drugs that had so long fueled his deluded notions of life. But spiritual deliverance in isolation did not have lasting appeal. For a while Douglas held onto his prideful position of not being a member of any organization or club. To be a Christian seemed right, but to be a member of a *church?* That idea made him squeamish. It seemed childish and degrading. After all, he could worship God just as well—or even better—in His natural cathedral, the woods, as in some stuffy building with stiff-backed pews.

But through continued Bible study and prayer Douglas discovered two things that changed his mind about church. First, Jesus taught plainly that *He* had established the church, and the gates of hell would not prevail against it. So church was of divine and not human origin. Once having seen this, Douglas was amazed by the frequent references to church in the New Testament. He saw that Christ had bought the church with His own blood, and that even though many problems in the church (including immorality, hypocrisy, materialism, and false teaching) were openly dealt with in the Bible, nowhere did Scripture indicate that the church as an institution was to be abolished because of these problems, but rather they were to be remedied in Christlike ways. This straightforward realism and practicality appealed to Douglas.

Then another change began to enter his thinking. As a potsmoking hippie, he had often craved the company of like-minded pleasure seekers. Usually he preferred being alone, yet from time to time Douglas sought out the company of those who liked the same kind of music, language, and ideas that he had chosen as a counter-culturist. He realized that no one can healthily live in isolation, but that all are called to serve and be served as part of a great social fabric. He began to hunger for fellowship with people who loved Jesus and valued His Word enough to live by its teachings. And the Bible said that there are such people and they constitute His church!

Once having recognized this, Douglas tried out various Christian fellowships. He moved to San Francisco and found a job. Although he saw some good things in the churches he visited, he was disappointed by their vague and often unscriptural teachings. Worldly talk, dress, and lifestyles seemed too predominant in the churches.

Douglas wasn't so unrealistic as to expect uniform perfection in the church, but he was convinced, from his reading of Scripture, that God's church would have a focused sense of mission to evangelize the world, starting in the local community. He also expected that the church would faithfully be teaching God's Word without compromise. Beyond that he anticipated that the membership would be composed of a broad spectrum of adherents from the fervent to the flaccid. He expected that some members would be studious and some slothful, some devoted and some disgruntled—after all, wasn't it so at Corinth, Galatia, and some other New Testament churches? Didn't Jesus teach that the wheat and tares were to grow together until the harvest, which is the end of the world? But Douglas at least expected that the Bible should be faithfully taught in church, and that a notable proportion of the members would be serious about their professed beliefs and not be ashamed to acknowledge themselves as God's peculiar people, delighting in His way (Titus 2:14; 1 Peter 2:9).

He remembered the Earls, who had led him to Christ several years earlier. Although he now lived more than 200 miles away, they kept in touch with him, supplying him with study materials and a Bible, along with such excellent books as *The Desire of Ages* and *The Great Controversy*. Douglas was impressed by the Earls' simple lifestyle and spirit of sacrificial service. Finally one day he asked them what church they belonged to. When they told him the name of their denomination, Douglas was immediately struck with the impression that any church which would take such an unusual name— Seventh-day Adventist—must have the courage of its convictions.

He started attending the nearest Adventist church in San Francisco, and to his delight found that the Sabbath school studies were about Revelation. Galvanized by the power of these lessons that exalted Christ as the Lamb of God and showed how He prepares people for heaven and triumphs over all evil, Douglas gave his life to Christ with new commitment. Not many months later, with convictions fully crystallized and his conversion progressing, Brian Douglas Jones became a baptized member of that church. It is now his privilege to write a book on the Bible teachings about God's church. He prays that the Lord will guide him in this effort to offer solid encouragement not only to current members but also to those who are considering membership in God's remnant church.

Alienation, a sense of not belonging, has become an increasingly pervasive problem in our society for the past century and a half. This is understandable. Until the Industrial Revolution, which has merged into the explosive Technological Revolution, most of earth's population lived in small rural communities. Each person's social and economic role was clearly defined. People generally worked at the trades that their forebears had pursued for generations, or they worked at some other occupation to which they were apprenticed. Few people, except those who joined an army or navy and the privileged few who went to college, moved far from their birthplace. Consequently their life's round of activities was fairly stable and routine.

But with the rapid changes brought about by science and industry, the population shift worldwide has been toward cities. People in general do not know their neighbors as former generations did. Employment is increasingly hard to find and of unstable duration. Many jobs are becoming obsolete; emerging occupations demand ever-increasing skills that fewer and fewer people can afford the means to obtain. We live in a time of rapid change that unsettles all but the most lethargic and the most courageous.

But in the midst of life's rapidly shifting scene, Someone does not change. That Someone is God (Mal. 3:6). Also, His purposes and values do not change. From the creation of our world (though veiled in the depths of His heart from eternity) God's everlasting gospel has drawn into sanctified fellowship all whom He can attract to Himself and His truth. "From the beginning, faithful souls have constituted the church on earth" *(The Acts of the Apostles,* p. 11). In its fullest sense, God's church consists of all His faithful followers who have ever lived on earth, uniting with all the worshipful beings in the universe (Eph. 3:10, 15, 21). Yet, as we shall see in later chapters, this does not blur the truth that God has a specific church on earth, which in a special sense constitutes His people in a world that largely rejects Him.

What are the features that specifically denote the people whom God calls His church? First and foremost they are a people who have subscribed to His covenant. His covenant was established in the Garden of Eden, when Adam and Eve sinned. It consisted of a promise to send a Saviour who would break the power of sin by which God's new race of beings had been foolishly ensnared (Gen. 3:15). In that promise was enfolded a prophecy of Christ's atoning sacrifice and the decreed end of Satan's existence and power. The knowledge of God's plan of redemption was transmitted reliably from generation to generation by those who called on His name, acknowledging His Lordship in their lives (see Gen. 4:26).

But sad to say, despite all God's mercy and guidance, the infection of willful sin continued its baleful work, and humanity became increasingly corrupt. Even those who had the knowledge of God were seduced by the fatal attractions of sin (Gen. 6:1, 2). The collective rebellion of humanity threatened to extinguish the light of truth in our world. God's diagnosis of the human condition was that people's thoughts were "only evil continually" (verse 5).

In mercy He sent a message of warning and loving invitation through Noah, a preacher of righteousness, who built an ark according to God's express command. Noah pleaded with people to repent and take refuge in the ark from the coming Flood (verses 5-13; Heb. 11:7; 2 Peter 2:5).

Of all living just prior to the Flood, only Noah and his family remained faithful and entered the ark. These small visible results for his labors were not because Noah's life and preaching lacked truth and conviction, but because the whole world was steeped in spiritual rebellion and selfish absorption in life's material blessings, without any gratitude or loyalty to the Creator (Matt. 24:37-39). Those who entered the ark with Noah constituted God's church,

His people, called out from the evils of the world and gathered into His ark of safety (1 Peter 3:18-21).

After destroying earth's rebellious population by a flood, the Lord gave this remnant of believers opportunity to make a fresh start. He created the rainbow as a token of His covenant of peace, a beautiful reminder not only that He would never again send a world-wide flood, but also that His kindness would never depart from humanity (Gen. 9:8-17; Isa. 54:9, 10). Many waters could not quench God's love; neither could the floods drown it (Song of Sol. 8:7).

But scarcely had the floodwaters subsided when Ham, one of Noah's sons, disgraced his father through immoral conduct (Gen. 9:22, 23). Nor was it long before the descendants of Noah indulged the same spirit of rebellious antagonism to God that had dominated the world before the Flood. This general apostasy and rebellion culminated in the building of the Tower of Babel, a project that represented humanity's flagrant defiance of God's word.

Desiring to check the progress of evil, God had commanded the people to spread over the earth and repopulate it in small communities in which individuals would be more accountable to one another, their work wholesome, and artificial diversions few. One leading motive for their defying this plan and building the Tower of Babel was to ensure their safety and protection in the event that God should break His word and cause another global deluge. The builders of this grand skyscraper wanted to make a name for themselves and peer into the mysteries of science by their own ingenuity and prowess without need for humble dependence on their Creator (Gen. 11:1-6; *Patriarchs and Prophets*, p. 119). In this grand undertaking, independence from God was their foremost objective.

For their own good, the Lord broke up this enterprise by dividing the languages of all who participated in the construction of the tower. Those who could understand one another banded together and moved to various parts of the world, each tribe establishing its own culture and customs, yet no tribe being without the basic light of truth (Acts 17:24-29). This accounts for the remarkable similarity of diverse tribal legends and myths that reveal a dimly preserved knowledge of historic and spiritual truths that are clearly and accurately recorded in Scripture.

But God was not content merely to have sketchy approximations of His truth survive. He longed that everywhere people should behold Him as He is (Isa. 65:1) and that they should have a clear understanding of His will in every matter that would contribute to their restored fellowship with Him (Num. 14:21; Hab. 2:14; 3:3, 4). Only 10 generations after the Flood (count them in Genesis 11:1-27), few of earth's once more teeming population were faithful to God. One man stood out among the rest as God's most faithful friend—Abram, the son of Terah, in Ur of the Chaldees. To Abram, whose name God changed to Abraham (father of many nations; see Gen. 17:1-7) the Lord disclosed His covenant of grace. He also promised Abraham that his descendants would dwell in the fertile land of Canaan, a land grant to His nation that would keep the truth. Israel was to become that nation. Any person of whatever nationality, if willing to subscribe fully to God's covenant, was free to join this elect nation (Isa. 56:1-8).

In a later chapter we shall see why national Israel, in its role as God's representative people, gave way to the Christian church. But now we simply note that in every age, including our own, God's church is composed of those who accept His covenant. This covenant, ratified with Christ's blood, offers pardon, peace, purity, and restored fellowship with God through the grace of Jesus (Matt. 20:28; 26:28; Heb. 8:10-12).

God establishes the terms of the covenant; it could not be the product of joint negotiations between God and humanity, because no human being could possibly conceive of the infinite treasures of love and moral elevation embodied in His covenant. Nor could human beings in their fallen state grasp the depth of ruin from which God's blood-sealed covenant redeems us. This covenant is not a merely formal document, but a relational bond. So rich and glorious are its provisions that only those who truly revere God can appreciate His covenant with us. "The secret of the Lord is with those who fear Him, and He will show them His covenant" (Ps. 25:14, NKJV).

In addition to, or rather as a natural result of, accepting Christ's covenant, God's people congregate to worship Him. Their fellowship is distinguished by love, unselfishness, willing service, and mutual trust as they unite their resources and talents to take the gospel to the world so that Christ's body, the church, might constantly increase in membership (Eph. 4:15, 16). This is not for the sake of organizational aggrandizement, but to bring as many as possible into a saving relationship with Jesus. By being active, dedicated members of God's church, we can join with other believers to work sensitively and effectively for the salvation of our communities.

"To human agencies is committed the work of extending the triumphs of the cross from point to point. As the Head of the church, Christ is authoritatively calling upon everyone who claims to believe on Him to follow His example of self-denial and self-sacrifice in working for the conversion of those whom Satan and his vast army are exerting every power to destroy. . . . When church members put forth earnest efforts to advance the message, they will live in the joy of the Lord and will meet with success. Triumph always follows decided effort" (*Testimonies,* vol. 7, p. 30).

I am grateful that the Earls believed this statement and that it inspired them to labor diligently for my salvation. I am grateful for all God's missionaries who are laboring for the salvation of multitudes who would otherwise never hear the gospel (Rom. 10:14, 15). I am grateful for faithful church members in every land who quietly but devotedly work to bring the light of truth to as many people as they can. I am grateful to belong to a church in which love for Christ and His Word and the souls for whom He died flourishes increasingly as we approach the end of time.

This work of active participation with Christ for the spread of His gospel and the resulting enlargement of His family is precious in His sight. It is the work to which He is committed and to which He calls each member of His church. Those who share in this work may evoke scorn and pity from worldly minds, but in heaven they are regarded in an altogether different light.

God declares with inspiring assurance: "Those who are wise shall shine like the brightness of the firmament, and those who turn many to righteousness like the stars forever and ever" (Dan. 12:3, NKJV).

Pilgrims and Strangers

2

It is interesting to read the biographies of people who have risen from obscurity to accomplish a work that benefits humanity. Their success is rarely, if ever, accidental. With few exceptions they hungered to be better people than they were. They harbored ideals that motivated them to persevere, even though no one else may have had confidence in them or their dreams. They wanted to make a difference and had no satisfaction with the status quo. This holds true in the heroes of both religious and secular life.

Christ's grace awakens dissatisfaction in our sinful hearts, dissatisfaction with ourselves, and dissatisfaction with the immoral, selfish atmosphere of the world. But the Spirit does more than generate discontentment with ungodliness. He arouses within us a hunger and thirst for righteousness—for purity, truth, and love. Few fully yield to these gracious influences, although many people cherish them vaguely as an ideal, impossible to attain except, perhaps, in some glorious hereafter. In every age, however, a few people are not satisfied with such vapid mysticism, but allow God to implant in their hearts a vision of the rich benefits attainable in this present world through His gospel (1 Cor. 15:1, 2, 34; Titus 2:11-14).

Such a man was Abraham. He could not be satisfied with the status quo of idolatrous, worldly living that surrounded him in Ur of the Chaldees, a city near modern Baghdad. Not that Abraham was self-righteous or holier-than-thou in his attitude. But his heart heard the music of God's love, the grandeur of His purpose for humanity. Descended from Shem, Abraham belonged to a tribe that still had some vestiges of regard for the Lord's plan to restore humanity to the image of God through the atonement.

Abraham was not a mere visionary. He did not have to create glorious dreams for the future, but rather was guided by the light of God's prophetic purpose. He looked for a city that had foundations, whose builder and maker was God (Heb. 11:10). External glory alone did not dazzle Abraham. His heart was drawn to the holiness, purity, and love of God. Recognizing his need of a Saviour, he saw that the idol worship and human philosophy which prevailed in his day were obstacles to true redemption. Unashamed of his faith, Abraham made no effort to hide his direct dependence on God for salvation. He worshiped God according to revealed truth. Abraham knew and loved the gospel (John 8:56; Gal. 3:8). Thus God was able to make him a blessing to the world (Gen. 12:2, 3).

Abraham's faith in God and his fixed loyalty to His word qualified him to be the forefather of God's chosen people Israel, whose distinctiveness depended on obedient faith in their self-revealing Lord. These qualities in Abraham made him also the divinely chosen pattern of faith for all time. He is named the "father of all them that believe" (Rom. 4:11). Implicit faith in God and obedience to His Word distinguish God's children in every age. Theirs is the righteousness of faith. They cast aside the idea of achieving righteousness through the law (verses 13-16; Phil. 3:9), because such "righteousness" is a futile sham, a desperate failure. It usually breeds complacency or frustration about one's self and contempt for others. And it stumbles badly over the freely offered grace of Christ, who alone can make us righteous (Rom. 9:30-33; 2 Cor. 5:20, 21).

While Abraham's faith in Christ as his Saviour was so deep and genuine that the Lord accounted it to him for righteousness, yet he never made the fatal assumption that faith excused him from obeying God's law. Rather, he recognized that by faith alone can God's law be kept, and he was conscientious in his observance of that law (Gen. 18:17-19; 22:16-18; 26:4, 5). Had it been otherwise, his faith and character would have had no more substance than cotton candy. After all, faith is an appropriative power that enables us to conform fully to God's teachings and plan for our lives, and that plan always includes our living unselfishly to honor God and benefit others.

18

Faith yields the good fruit of obedient action. James asserted this fact in masterstrokes of irrefutable logic, citing Abraham's experience to illustrate the point: "What does it profit, my brethren, if someone says he has faith but does not have works? Can faith save him? If a brother or sister is naked and destitute of daily food, and one of you says to them, 'Depart in peace, be warmed and filled,' but you do not give them the things which are needed for the body, what does it profit? Thus also faith by itself, if it does not have works, is dead. But someone will say, 'You have faith, and I have works.' Show me your faith without your works, and I will show you my faith by my works. You believe that there is one God. You do well. Even the demons believe—and tremble! But do you want to know, O foolish man, that faith without works is dead? Was not Abraham our father justified by works when he offered Isaac his son on the altar? Do you see that faith was working together with his works, and by works faith was made perfect? And the Scripture was fulfilled which says, 'Abraham believed God, and it was accounted to him for righteousness.' And he was called the friend of God. You see then that a man is justified by works, and not by faith only. . . . For as the body without the spirit is dead, so faith without works is dead also" (James 2:14-26, NKJV).

James is not undercutting the doctrine of righteousness by faith here, but affirming that true faith is *lived.* It expresses itself in Christlike actions of love and honest obedience to God's will. His teaching harmonizes with Paul's statement: "For not the hearers of the law are just in the sight of God, but the doers of the law will be justified" (Rom. 2:13, NKJV). John echoes this position in his own pointed way: "My little children, let us not love in word or in tongue, but in deed and in truth" (1 John 3:18, NKJV).

Faith that doesn't do what God requires has as much value as pictures of food sent to starving people, or as prayer wheels turning in the wind. True faith *works by love* (Gal. 5:6). Works of obedience result from faith. They are not added to it as a supplement or prop.

Abraham's obedient faith made him brave, benevolent, and venturesome to follow the Lord where others dared not go. By faith Abraham left his idolatrous land to journey where God directed. By faith he embraced in his old age the promise of a son; by faith he rescued Lot and the captives of Sodom from the marauding kings; by faith he interceded for Sodom; by faith he offered up his son Isaac according to God's command. By faith he recognized the sacrifice of Christ on Calvary when God spared Isaac. By faith Abraham sent Eliezer to discover a godly wife for Isaac. By faith he kept his gaze on the heavenly kingdom. By faith he served the Lord as the spiritual father of the faithful in all subsequent ages. One day these spiritual descendants, along with all who were faithful before Abraham, will compose the entire family of the redeemed.

One aspect of Abraham's witness of faith is especially worthy of our consideration in today's world—his family life. "God called Abraham to be a teacher of His word, He chose him to be the father of a great nation, because He saw that Abraham would instruct his children and his household in the principles of God's law. And that which gave power to Abraham's teaching was the influence of his own life. His great household consisted of more than a thousand souls, many of them heads of families, and not a few but newly converted from heathenism. Such a household required a firm hand at the helm. No weak, vacillating methods would suffice. Of Abraham God said, 'I know him, that he will command his children and his household after him.' Gen. 18:19. Yet his authority was exercised with such wisdom and tenderness that hearts were won. The testimony of the divine Watcher is, 'They shall keep the way of the Lord, to do justice and judgment.' Gen. 18:19" *(Education,* p. 187).

Closely connected with his godly home life was Abraham's active service in sharing his faith with others. "During their stay in Haran, both Abraham and Sarah had led others to the worship and service of the true God. These attached themselves to the patriarch's household, and accompanied him to the land of promise. . . .

"Abraham, 'the friend of God,' set us a worthy example. His was a life of prayer. Wherever he pitched his tent, close beside it was set up his altar, calling all within his encampment to the morning and evening sacrifice. . . . There were those among the roving Canaanites who received instruction from Abraham . . . , and [in consequence] worshiped the living God" *(Patriarchs and Prophets,* pp. 127, 128).

We can see then that Abraham was a missionary. He did not view his religion as a closely held tribal cult, because he clearly understood the universality of God's plan for the world. He worshiped

God, the Creator of all, and realized that as a worshiper of the true God, he had a duty to reveal the way of truth to all. This he was to do not by some great pageantry or display, but by his teachings, character, and practices. While this responsibility called for a consecrated life and unwavering commitment, it ruled out all prideful exclusiveness that would make Abraham's God seem cold, distant, and unapproachable.

Abraham's communicative, outgoing faith sets the example for all who worship God in spirit and in truth. "Christ's church is to be a blessing, and its members are to be blessed as they bless others. The object of God in choosing a people before all the world was not only that He might adopt them as His sons and daughters, but that through them He might confer on the world the benefits of divine illumination. When the Lord chose Abraham it was not simply to be the special friend of God, but to be a medium of the precious and peculiar privileges the Lord desired to bestow upon the nations. He was to be a light amid the moral darkness of his surroundings" *(Reflecting Christ*, p. 205).

Before we pass on from this consideration of Abraham's calling as the father of the faithful, we should note his lapses from faith. Scripture does not present Abraham as a flawless example of trustful dependence. Abraham's history is not a fairy tale, but an instructive biography from which we should learn what mistakes to avoid as well as what virtues to adopt. Twice Abraham concealed the fact that Sarah was his wife, and for self-preserving reasons simply called her his sister (which was only half the truth) and nothing more. For this prevarication God's honor and Abraham's witness were seriously compromised (Gen. 12:11-20; 20). Abraham's laughter at God's renewed promise of a son exhibited a lack of faith in His stated plan (Gen. 17:17). And Abraham's unwise capitulation to Sarah's pressure to use her servant Hagar as the only possible means of bearing the son of promise resulted in lasting trouble to millions in future ages (Gen. 16:6-12).

In the face of this disturbing record, cold narrow reason would write Abraham off as a poor, inconsistent example of faith. But Scripture gives a far different appraisal of him. The Lord's ultimate testimony about Abraham is that he "against hope believed in hope, that he might become the father of many nations; according to that which was spoken, So shall thy seed be. And being not weak in faith, he considered not his own body now dead, when he was about a hundred years old, neither yet the deadness of Sara's womb: *he staggered not at the promise of God through unbelief; but was strong in faith, giving glory to God;* and being fully persuaded that, what he had promised, he was able also to perform. And therefore it was imputed to him for righteousness" (Rom. 4:18-22).

What a remarkable conclusion! How seemingly at odds with the facts. And yet the testimony in Romans is true, because God is not emphasizing Abraham's failures, but the eventual recovery and triumph of his faith. Abraham's ultimate experience was not one of self-defeat but of victory in Christ.

That victory did not come without an excruciating test. "God had called Abraham to be the father of the faithful, and his life was to stand as an example of faith to succeeding generations. But his faith had not been perfect. . . . That he might reach the highest standard, God subjected him to another test, the closest which man was ever called to endure" *(Patriarchs and Prophets*, p. 147).

God called upon Abraham to sacrifice Isaac, the son of promise, whose descendants were to be as numerous as the stars. With unutterable grief but resolute faith, Abraham moved to carry out the mysterious, heartbreaking command. His faith found its center and stability in the assurance that God would provide Himself a lamb. Abraham was willing to obey the divine mandate, believing in God's ability and willingness to restore Isaac to life (see Heb. 11:17-19). But before Abraham could consummate the sacrifice, God interposed. The ram that He provided in place of Isaac symbolized Christ, who centuries later laid down His life for our salvation and "was raised again for our justification" (Rom. 4:25; see also Gen. 22:1-18).

In this the most crucial test of his life, Abraham grasped the victory, because without a shadow of reservation or lingering doubt, he made God his reliance. Thus his past failures were redeemed—not by works, but by faith that was so real it remained actively and victoriously obedient to God to meet the supreme test.

Abraham provides a bracing example for us all. Days of dark crisis await God's family on earth. The faith of every believing, obedient child of God will be tried to the uttermost (see Matt.

24:21-25). Like Abraham, all of us have failed God in ways that have hurt others and dishonored His name. But the Lord does not wish to seal up the record of our lives with a humiliating testimony of disappointment and loss. He wishes rather to summarize our experience with this declaration: "Here is the patience of the saints: here are they that keep the commandments of God, and the faith of Jesus" (Rev. 14:12).

We don't need to cling to defeat when it is our privilege to grasp victory through the faith of Jesus, exercised in simple adherence to His Word and continuance in the fellowship of His Spirit.

Do you wish to have a victorious faith to the end? Then remember Abraham's experience of active, obedient faith that refused to give up, even in the face of his own stunning failures. Abraham's faith was not in his own faith, but in God's faithfulness.

Such an enduring, dauntless faith Christ is ready to give us, because He is the author and finisher of our faith. He longs for the day when He can say to all who triumph through the faith of Jesus: "Well done, good and faithful servants: . . . enter into the joy of your Lord" (Matt. 25:21, adapted).

"And if you are Christ's, then you are Abraham's seed, and heirs according to the promise" (Gal. 3:29, NKJV).

A Kingdom
of Priests

3

Little Princess Wilhelmina, destined to be queen of the Netherlands, was riding in a coach with her grandmother. They proceeded in stately fashion along a broad boulevard lined on both sides with patriotic Dutch who came to admire the royal passengers. Wilhelmina, delirious with joy over the admiring cheers of the people, burst out, "Oh, Grandmamma, do all these people belong to me?"

Soberly but kindly her grandmother replied, "No, my dear. You belong to all these people."

This illustrates a basic truth the Lord wished His people Israel to understand about their royal calling and election in Him. He purposed that they should be a nation of kings and priests, not so that they could dominate the world or stand regally aloof from it, but so that all humanity might be blessed and ennobled by their witness. And yet it was imperative that they remain in certain ways distinctly separate from the world. Like Abraham, their forefather, the Jews were to keep clear of the pollutions of heathendom and sensual living. This was not to maintain an impassable gulf between themselves and other nations, but rather to build a bridge over which people from every nation and culture could pass as they made their own exodus from gross darkness into the marvelous light of the gospel, whose power and glory they were to see displayed in Israel (see Isa. 60-62; Micah 4:2; John 4:22).

As we have seen from previous chapters, God's covenant with Israel was the foundation not only of their national existence, but of their individual faith as well. At least that was God's intention. His

24

covenant with Israel was designed as a remedial system to bring lost humanity back into harmony with God. This restoration involved not only obedience to God's law, but also restored fellowship with Him.

See how beautifully this idea is expressed in God's message to Israel through Moses: "Thus shall you say to the house of Jacob, and tell the children of Israel: 'You have seen . . . how I bore you on eagles' wings and brought you to Myself. Now therefore, if you will indeed obey My voice and keep My covenant, then you shall be a special treasure to Me above all people; for all the earth is Mine. And you shall be to Me a kingdom of priests and a holy nation.' These are the words which you shall speak to the children of Israel" (Ex. 19:3-6, NKJV).

With sincere but unperceptive confidence, the people of Israel declared: "All that the Lord has spoken we will do" (verse 8). Their well-meaning but hasty vow had four problems:

1. They had no conception of their natural inability to obey.

2. They had a very limited conception of Christ's righteousness and love.

3. They lacked insight into the true meaning of obedience.

4. They utterly failed to grasp the beauty and value of fellowship with God. They saw Him primarily as an overlord rather than as a loving shepherd, companion, Saviour, and friend. (See these four points indicated in Romans 9:30-10:1.)

They were right to acknowledge God's Lordship; to fail in this point would have been irreverent. But to see Him as Lord *only* and not also as a loving friend makes obedience to Him impossible (Deut. 30:6, 8-20; Isa. 26:12, 13; John 15:5; Phil. 4:13).

After God proclaimed the Ten Commandments on Sinai and revealed to Moses some specific applications of the moral law, He affirmed His covenant with the children of Israel. Again they repeated their self-confident assertion: "All that the Lord has said we will do, and be obedient" (Ex. 24:7, NKJV). When Moses sprinkled ox blood on the altar, on the book of the covenant, and on the people themselves and said, "Behold the blood of the covenant, which the Lord hath made with you concerning all these words," little did they grasp the significance of His action (verse 8). The sprinkled blood testified that only through God's atoning sacrifice could they receive pardon and cleansing for sin and spiritual grace to obey Him. Only through grace applied could they know God and serve Him acceptably. The symbolism was not so veiled and obscure that they could not have understood it. The book of Hebrews states that the gospel was preached to the children of Israel under Moses (Heb. 4:2).

In a certain sense the Lord never did make an "old" covenant with Israel, at least not in the sense of teaching them that they could be justified by their own works of righteousness in compliance with the law (see Joshua 24:19-24). Rather, the teaching of righteousness by faith was richly embedded and graphically depicted in the ceremonial law.

This covenant was *old* not because it taught righteousness by works, but because it portrayed only in emblematic terms the provisions of the atonement. It presented the shadow and not the substance of Christ's sacrifice. Yet those who by faith were looking beyond the shadow to the reality typified in the ceremonial law had a new covenant experience. This is evident from such Old Testament passages as Deuteronomy 30; Psalms 22, 32, and 51; Isaiah 53; Jeremiah 31:31-34; Ezekiel 34:11-16; 36:25-29; Daniel 9; Hosea 14; Micah 7:7-9, 18-20; Habakkuk 3:1-4, 17-19; Zechariah 12:10-13:1; and Malachi 3:1-6. Down through the centuries of Israel's existence, the truth tolled like a mighty bell. "It is the blood that maketh an atonement for the soul" (Lev. 17:11)—not the repenting believer's blood, but the blood of the sacrifice typifying the Messiah's atoning death.

When Christ died on Calvary, He caused the need for the ceremonial law to cease, as His word had foretold centuries before (Dan. 9:27; cf. Matt. 27:50, 51; 1 Peter 1:10-12). The rituals of the sanctuary service, while they movingly portrayed Christ's sacrifice and the way to appropriate its merits, were nonetheless a burdensome imposition, as the Scriptures clearly state (Heb. 9:10; 10:8-10; cf. Deut. 31:24-26). After all, what delight could be taken in the sacrificial slaughter of innocent animals?

While the ceremonial law is forever ended, it is still a profitable subject to study because it symbolically portrays the inner workings of the plan of salvation (see, for example, Heb. 8-10). The whole book of Revelation is saturated with the imagery of the Hebrew sanctuary service, and thus the study of this subject as presented in the Old Testament continues to be valuable in the highest degree. "Thy way, O God, is in the sanctuary" (Ps. 77:13; cf. Ps. 20:1, 2; 43:3; 63:2). The subject is soul-strengthening and large with majesty. "In his temple everything saith, Glory" (Ps. 29:9, ASV).

The old covenant was designed to elicit a heart response. "In the way of thy judgments, O Lord, have we waited for thee; the desire of our soul is to thy name, and to the remembrance of thee" (Isa. 26:8; cf. Ps. 73:23-26). With ineffably deep yearning the Lord cried out: "Oh, that they had such a heart in them that they would fear Me and always keep all My commandments, that it might be well with them and with their children forever!" (Deut. 5:29, NKJV; cf. Isa. 48:16-18).

True religion from eternity past to eternity future is ever an affair of the heart. It has never merely consisted of outward compliance with coldly prescribed duties.

Samuel Rutherford, a dissenting pastor of seventeenth-century Scotland, enjoyed a sublime and intimate fellowship with God that gave power to his ministry. While staying at a friend's house, he was observed by the maid, who saw him slowly pacing about his room. Looking heavenward with rapture and longing on his face, he uttered a threefold petition to the Lord. First he cried out with intense yearning, "Lord, make me believe in Thee!" He paused, sat down, and was lost in meditation. Then he arose, and now his cry was "Lord, make me love Thee!" After waiting a minute or two, he entreated with breaking voice, "Lord, make me to keep all Thy commandments!"

Belief, love, and obedience—all exercised through God's enabling power—are the three qualities that impart vital force to the worshiper's experience. Both before and after Calvary, only those who have taken in the rich significance of Christ's "new" commandment of love have really had a new covenant experience (see John 13:34; 1 John 2:4-10).

Had Israel as a nation grasped the soul-regenerating power of God's covenant with them, they would truly have been the light of the world (Deut. 4:4-13; Isa. 49:3-6). Until national Israel's conclusive rejection of the Messiah, the potential was always present for their spiritual influence to blossom forth in fruitfulness that would have encompassed the world with heaven's glory (Isa. 27:5;

60:1-5; 62:1-7). To a limited extent in their history Israel did this during a few golden seasons of ripe responsiveness to God (Num. 23:20-24; 1 Kings 10:1-9, 24; 2 Chron. 32:22, 23).

From their beginning as a nation, God revealed to Israel that they were to naturalize as one with themselves all Gentiles who willingly subscribed to His covenant (Ex. 12:48, 49; Num. 15:14-16, 29). God's universal plan of salvation through the coming Messiah found increasingly rich expression through the Hebrew prophets over the centuries as the time of Christ's advent drew near (e.g., Deut. 32:43; Ps. 117; Isa. 19:18-25; 42:6; 49:8, 9; 56:1-7; 60:1-11; Eze. 47:22, 23; Dan. 9:24-27; Amos 9:7, 11, 12; Micah 4:1, 2; Hab. 2:14; 3:3, 4; Haggai 2:7).

A careful study of the Old Testament in comparison with the New reveals how closely the Lord has always tied the universality of His plan of salvation to the sanctuary. For instance, He declared that His house was to be a house of prayer for all people (Isa. 56:7; cf. 2 Chron. 6:28-33), and that eventually all nations would come up to "the house of the God of Jacob" (sanctuary) to learn the ways of God (Micah 4:2). Of course this does not mean that most of humanity would accept the Lord, but that responsive people from every nation, kindred, and tongue would learn and accept the truth that God had anciently revealed to the Jews and had so richly embodied in His sanctuary services, all pointing forward to Christ's sacrifice and high priestly work in the heavenly tabernacle (Heb. 8:1-6; 9:1-15; 1 John 2:1, 2; Rev. 1:10-20; 11:19; 14:6; 22:16, 17; cf. Eze. 47:1-12).

"God desired to make of His people Israel a praise and a glory. Every spiritual advantage was given them. God withheld from them nothing favorable to the formation of character that would make them representatives of Himself.

"Their obedience to the law of God would make them marvels of prosperity before the nations of the world. He who could give them wisdom and skill in all cunning work would continue to be their teacher, and would ennoble and elevate them through obedience to His laws. . . . The glory of God [His character], His majesty and power, were to be revealed in all their prosperity. They were to be a kingdom of priests and princes. God furnished them with every facility for becoming the greatest nation on earth. . . .

"It was God's purpose that by the revelation of His character through Israel men should be drawn unto Him. To all the world the gospel invitation was to be given. Through the teaching of the sacrificial service Christ was to be uplifted before the nations, and all who would look unto Him should live. All who, like Rahab the Canaanite, and Ruth the Moabitess, turned from idolatry to the worship of the true God, were to unite themselves with His chosen people. As the numbers of Israel increased they were to enlarge their borders, until their kingdom should embrace the world" *(Christ's Object Lessons,* pp. 288-290).

Israel sometimes mingled with the surrounding nations, not to benefit them spiritually but rather to absorb their immoral customs and form forbidden alliances that corrupted their own worship (Judges 3:5-7; Ps. 106:34-39). For several generations prior to Christ's first advent, the religious leaders of Israel, as a check against pagan influence, directed their people into a program of rigid exclusiveness and isolation from the Gentile conquerors who occupied their land. Thus Jews and Gentiles became increasingly antagonistic and mistrustful toward one another. The Jewish religion crystallized into self-protective ceremonialism that lost sight of the compassionate, redeeming purposes of their prophetic teachings and whole system of worship. Thus Israel, falling sadly short of its calling and privileges, forfeited its commission as God's holy nation that would enlighten the earth with His glory. Christ transferred this honor and duty to His church (Matt. 21:43).

On the surface Israel's sad record of apostasy and rebellion looks like a singular example of spiritual blindness and ingratitude that no other people could ever repeat. But then we read this sobering admonition: "All these things happened to them as examples for others, and they were written down as a warning for us. For we live at a time when the end is about to come. Whoever thinks he is standing firm had better be careful that he does not fall" (1 Cor. 10:11, 12, TEV).

The Christian church, including the remnant, has also fallen astonishingly short of its privileges and responsibilities. In Scripture God repeatedly admonishes us to cleave to Him and His Word. Our power as His professed people resides in maintaining a living union with Him and a love for His Word that exhibits itself in obedience to His will.

Those who do not part company with Christ and His truth do not apostatize. Just as ancient Israel was guarded and preserved by the cumulative testimony of her prophets, past and present, so the church is to be guarded today (see 2 Chron. 20:20; Hosea 12:10). The Bible is the foundational testimony by which all ideas and experience are tested, and God's spiritual gifts are to be found in healthy exercise among us, to produce sanctified harmony and vibrant growth in our fellowship (1 Cor. 1:4-10; Eph. 4:8-16).

The gifts and calling of God are without retraction on His part (Rom. 11:29). And His covenant with Israel is eternal (Jer. 31:31-37; 32:37-40). Who, then, is the Israel of God today? Who are the people who constitute His holy nation? *Those who keep His truth in new covenant relations; those whose hearts are united to fear His name; those in whom Christ lives and moves and has His being to make them a blessing to the world, even as Abraham was.*

The Lord knows those who are His. Wherever they are and whatever their nationality, they constitute the true Israel of God (Phil. 3:3; 2 Tim. 2:9). But this does not exhaust the subject. Christ purposes that His people shall be gathered into one united flock, the church that keeps His commandments and has the faith of Jesus (Isa. 56:8; John 10:16; Rev. 14:1-5, 12).

Wheat and tares—the truehearted and the false—eventually, through the work of the Holy Spirit, are winnowed out. False believers shall be shaken out, while the genuine followers of Christ remain in His church (Isa. 4:3, 4; 52:1, 2; Matt. 3:11, 12). They joyfully accept the power of His promises, the legitimacy of His requirements, and the blessings of His fellowship.

To understand the New Testament concept of spiritual Israel is to be fortified against a multitude of doctrinal errors. A failure to understand this subject has led many to conclude erroneously that God's moral law was for the Jews only, that political Israel shall be the final proclaimer of the gospel to the world, and that the destiny of nations is bound up in their relations with that country. But such texts as John 1:47; Romans 2:28, 29; 9:6-8; 10:11-13; and Hebrews 8:10-12 affirm that all born-again Christians, who obey the divine law, constitute the true Israel of God. Nationality is immaterial. "For we are the circumcision, who worship God in the Spirit, and rejoice in Christ Jesus, and have no confidence in the flesh" (Phil. 3:3, NKJV; cf. Gal. 3:28, 29).

Still, God's Word holds forth mighty hope that many who are natural descendants of Abraham shall come to the Lord in these closing days. After all, the final proclamation of the gospel, with all truth fully restored, presents the consummation of Judaism. (See Rom. 10:1-3; 11:7-32; cf. Hosea 2:14-23; 3:4, 5; Amos 9:11-15.) We cannot give here the detailed consideration that these passages deserve, but Ellen White offers valuable insight into their implications.

"There is a mighty work to be done in our world. The Lord declares that the Gentiles shall be gathered in, and not the Gentiles only, but the Jews. There are among the Jews many who will be converted, and through whom we shall see the salvation of God go forth as a lamp that burneth. There are Jews everywhere, and to them the light of present truth is to be brought. There are among them many who will come to the light, and who will proclaim the immutability of the law of God with wonderful power. . . .

"Among the Jews are some who, like Saul of Tarsus, are mighty in the Scriptures, and these will proclaim with wonderful power the immutability of the law of God. The God of Israel will bring this to pass in our day. As His servants labor in faith for those who have long been neglected and despised, His salvation will be revealed.

"When this gospel shall be presented in its fulness to the Jews, many will accept Christ as the Messiah" *(About Work for the Jewish People*, pp. 5, 6).

"The slumbering faculties of the Jewish people are to be aroused. The Old Testament scriptures, blending with the New, will be to them as the dawning of a new creation, or as the resurrection of the soul. Memory will be awakened as Christ is seen portrayed in the pages of the Old Testament. Souls will be saved, from the Jewish nation, as the doors of the New Testament are unlocked with the key of the Old Testament. Christ will be recognized as the Saviour of the world, as it is seen how clearly the New Testament explains the Old. Many of the Jewish people will by faith receive Christ as their Redeemer" *(Evangelism,* pp. 578, 579).

These Jewish converts in fellowship with all Gentile converts will make up the true Israel of God. "And so all Israel shall be saved" (Rom. 11:26; cf. Gal. 3:7-9, 28, 29).

Upon
This Rock

4

A self-proclaimed oracle named Bodhisattva (Enlightened One) Rob stood by a pond near the entrance to Golden Gate Park in San Francisco. His entourage of psychedelic devotees listened with fascination or blank bemusement as he held forth on a variety of mystical subjects, one of which was his claim to Messiahship. He insisted that he was not the ultimate Messiah but one of many, thus broadening the field of contenders for the role of redeemer.

Standing in the pond while holding a can of beer, I listened and wondered. The steady traffic along Stanyan Street only a few hundred feet outside the park became inaudible, and a mysterious stillness came over my mind. Maybe this pot-smoking, white-robed figure with lean body and long hair was a kind of messiah after all.

I was familiar with the idea of Hindu yogis who functioned as "saviors" of their disciples. The theory was that a yogi (or guru) would absorb the karma (moral consequences) of his followers' behavior and thus shorten their cycle of earthly sufferings as they progressed from one incarnation to another in their journey toward discarnate cosmic bliss. In other words, those who were finally freed from their karma would not have to live in a body anymore, but could be happy spirits, or else they could choose to incarnate as yogis for the salvation of others. At least this was one branch of Hindu thinking, and it appealed to my confused ideals.

But my guru ran off with his girlfriend, leaving his loosely knit followers to drift along on their journey without his transcendental guidance. It was a relief to have him gone. But that didn't end my search for redemption. I tried various other yogis in San Francisco and neighboring places, but obtained nothing of lasting value from any of them. Once while walking in Golden Gate Park, I saw Krishnamurti, a popular Hindu author, walking alone. I wanted to run up to him and seek some enlightenment from his lips, but his elegant European suit and polished shoes contrasted intimidatingly with my baggy outfit and scuffed footgear, so I let the opportunity slip by. And so I drifted on, foundationless for several more years, tossing on a sea of wistful hopes, delusive dreams, and deepening dissatisfaction with life as I knew it, but always craving love and inner cleansing.

And then the one true foundation was presented to me by some who were building on it. I discovered that on this foundation I could live and die without fear. *"Other foundation can no man lay than that is laid, which is Jesus Christ"* (1 Cor. 3:11). On this foundation I discovered His church, His embassy of truth and salvation to the world.

The church in the wilderness (Acts 7:38), Israel, grew to a populous nation under God's blessing. But most of them rejected the Messiah and worshiped their *religion* instead of their God. From the remnant of this holy nation the Christian church emerged. Its rise was amazing, because its charter members were 12 men of discordant temperaments and glaring faults. No seasoned personnel committee would have ever selected the apostles to launch so significant a movement as Christ envisioned, a church that was to evangelize the world with the fullness of God's glorious truth. Judas, because of his religious education, executive ability, and flair for self-promotion, might have been selected, but the other 11 were too unpolished, unstable, and unlearned to qualify for so high a calling—at least in human estimation.

What, then, was the secret of the apostles' power and the permanence of that movement to which they devoted their lives and for which most of them died as martyrs? The secret resides in their connection with the Founder of their faith, Jesus Christ, and their unshakable belief in His word.

As far as the religious leaders of Christ's time were concerned, His followers were running after a false messiah, a satanically gifted impostor, whom they contemptuously named Beelzebub (Mark 3:22), that is, "lord of the flies." But He was the King of heaven, the Lord of angels and all creation.

It was for love's sake that Christ came and for love's sake that He established His church (John 3:16; 1 John 4:7-9). He saw the vastness of its mission, which was to carry the light of the gospel to a world entangled in a dark web of sin, superstition, and false philosophy. Added to this difficulty is the internal warfare that goes on in every human heart between attraction and aversion to things divine.

John the Baptist by openly hailing Christ as the world's redeemer (John 1:29) bore witness to His true identity and mission, and at Christ's baptism the Father audibly proclaimed from heaven, "This is My beloved Son, in whom I am well pleased" (Matt. 3:17). It was necessary to establish Jesus' identity and promote a knowledge of it, because His authority is based on His being the promised Messiah of Scripture. As Messiah, He is God along with His Father. As God, His authority is absolute. And as God, His word is true, eternal, and paramount over all the words of humans, no matter how persuasively or learnedly the worldly-wise may contradict His words and reject His commandments. "Whoever transgresses and does not abide in the doctrine of Christ does not have God. He who abides in the doctrine of Christ has both the Father and the Son" (2 John 9, NKJV; see also Matthew 5:17-19; Luke 6:46; John 5:39-47; 8:31-37; 14:15, 21-24; 15:7, 14; 17:17; 20:31, which all emphasize the supreme importance of His word).

Christ knew how imperative it was for His disciples to acknowledge His Messiahship and its accompanying authority. They needed to recognize this in order to understand that His impending sacrifice was not some unforeseen calamity that aborted His mission, but the promised fulfillment of His age-old prophecy to give His life as a ransom for sinners. They also needed to recognize His Messiahship so that they would ascribe rightful supremacy to His instruction instead of their own opinions and doubts and all the erudite denial of the world's wisest instructors who claimed to be speaking for God.

So Christ asked them: "Whom do men say that I the Son of man am?" (Matt. 16:13). Many were willing to consider Him a prophet of God, but even this admission fell far short of the whole truth. No mere prophet, whether by the name of John the Baptist, Elijah, or Jeremiah, could save anyone's soul. At best they could point to the Saviour and faithfully relay His message through their tongues or pens. But only one Person could redeem any from sin—Christ, the promised Saviour.

This is why Peter's ringing declaration, "Thou art the Christ, the Son of the living God" (verse 16), drew such positive words of affirmation from Jesus: "Blessed art thou, Simon Bar-jona: for flesh and blood hath not revealed it unto thee, but my Father which is in heaven. And I say also unto thee, That thou art Peter, and upon this rock I will build my church; and the gates of hell shall not prevail against it" (verses 17, 18).

That Peter is not the Rock upon which the church is built is evident from his citation of scriptures that identify Christ as the chief cornerstone of the church and a rock of offense to His rejecters (see 1 Peter 2:6, 8; cf. Isa. 8:14; 28:16). Nor did the apostles then or at any future time relate to Peter as the foundation of the church. (For example, Acts 15—James, not Peter, presides at a general meeting of the churches; Galatians 2:11-16—Paul rebukes Peter for his cowardly dissimulation; 1 Peter 5:1, 3; 2 Peter 1:1—Peter calls himself *an* elder and *an* apostle, but not the supreme head of Christendom; instead he warns all against lording it over God's flock.) The Scriptures consistently identify the Rock as God Himself (Deut. 32:3, 4; Ps. 92:15; 1 Cor. 10:1-4).

"In the presence of God, and all the heavenly intelligences, in the presence of the unseen army of hell, Christ founded His church upon the living Rock. That Rock is Himself—His own body, for us broken and bruised. Against the church built upon this foundation, the gates of hell shall not prevail.

"How feeble the church appeared when Christ spoke these words! There was only a handful of believers, against whom all the power of demons and evil men would be directed; yet the followers of Christ were not to fear. Built upon the Rock of their strength, they could not be overthrown" *(The Desire of Ages*, p. 413).

Christ was so determined that His followers should base their faith on the evidences of His Word that following His resurrection Jesus hid His identity from two disconsolate disciples until He could reestablish their faith in Him on the teachings of Scripture (see Luke 24:13-32).

"Beginning at Moses, the very Alpha of Bible history, Christ expounded in all the Scriptures the things concerning Himself. Had

He first made Himself known to them, their hearts would have been satisfied. In the fullness of their joy they would have hungered for nothing more. But it was necessary for them to understand the witness borne to Him by the types and prophecies of the Old Testament. Upon these their faith must be established. Christ performed no miracle to convince them, but it was His first work to explain the Scriptures" *(ibid.,* pp. 796-799).

A clear knowledge of and complete faith in Scripture are of no less importance in our time than they were in the days of the early church. Those who truly know and love Scripture cannot be tossed about by every wind of doctrine that assails their ears. They learn to trust God's Word above their own imperfect reasoning powers. And they conscientiously base all their values on His teachings rather than on the changing customs and mores of the world. Moreover, they value and love the church as Christ does, despite its obvious flaws and shortcomings, for His word takes cognizance of those problems too (see, for example, Rev. 2 and 3).

So long as the church patterns its beliefs and actions after the precepts and example of Christ, it can never lose the distinctive character of its message, mission, and fellowship, all of which are to reflect the church's divine origin.

Christ bought the church with His own blood. Therefore it is infinitely precious in His eyes (Acts 20:28). The power of His cross in the message and lives of church members is the secret of the church's inexhaustible, ever-expanding influence (John 12:32; Eph. 2:16-19; Col. 1:20-23). The cross is the stanchless fount of every grace and gift that vitalizes the church. Church members, crucified with Christ—crucified to every unholy element of their natures, to everything selfish and vain—are free to live in full resurrection power and in that power colabor with Christ for the salvation of the world (Eph. 1:17-23).

Through the apostle Paul, Christ portrays the church as His body, with Himself as the head (verses 22, 23; Col. 1:17, 18). Therefore He is the source of the church's life, the fountainhead of its fellowship, the director of its mission, the preserver of its unity, integrity, and continuity of purpose (John 15:1-8). Without His headship over it, the church would have disintegrated centuries ago or would have degenerated into an unrecognizable mutation of its original design.

As members of His body, all church communicants are to work in harmony with Him and one another, or there is discord and disease in the body. A careful study of 1 Corinthians 12 reveals that God's Spirit fosters in the church rich diversity in a setting of unity.

The diversity of gifts and personalities found in the body of Christ enables it to serve all humanity with far greater effectiveness than would be possible if all believers were fashioned into a stereotyped similarity.

Christ's Spirit does not annihilate individuality, but accentuates and sublimates it to be a unique vehicle for the expression of His ministering love to the world. He invests every believer with a different combination of spiritual gifts to teach us humility, interdependence, trust, cooperation, mutual respect, and the spirit of service.

The gifts given to every believer find their fulfillment in being exercised for the practical and spiritual benefit of others. Gifts not used in this way deteriorate or depart (see Matt. 25:14-30; Luke 8:18). Never are spiritual gifts to be exploited as a vehicle for self-promotion; that is a profanation of their purpose. Consider the abuse of tongues in the Corinthian church. The egotistic, self-exalting use of this gift among them produced discord and chaos in their fellowship and, as Paul warned, could only make them look ridiculous to nonchristians who, on visiting their church, would see the Corinthian believers as a pack of wild exhibitionists frantically vying for attention (1 Cor. 14:23).

But the loving, unselfish use of spiritual gifts produces a heavenly fragrance that honors God and attracts honest people to Christ, the Giver of every gift and grace. Such was the influence of the believers at Colossae and Thessalonica (see Col. 1:3-12; 1 Thess. 1:2-10).

The presence of Christlike love in the hearts of believers gives the church immortality and compelling influence in the world (John 13:34; Eph. 4:15, 16). Love for Christ and humanity filled the hearts of the apostles and their converts. This love gave impetus and rich tone to their evangelistic efforts. Through their mutual love for Christ and each other, they always resolved whatever strife or discord arose among them. They did not permit cultural or temperamental differences to divide their ranks or jeopardize the sweet harmony of their fellowship.

Christ into all the world was their creed. And they marched

forth bravely under His banner not only to preach the truth, but to demonstrate attractively its power without resort to gimmicks, pretenses, or worldly inducements. "In the early church Christianity was taught in its purity; its precepts were given by the voice of inspiration; its ordinances were uncorrupted by the device of men. The church revealed the spirit of Christ and appeared beautiful in its simplicity. Its adorning was the holy principles and exemplary lives of its members. Multitudes were won to Christ, not by display or learning, but by the power of God which attended the plain preaching of His word" *(Testimonies,* vol. 5, p. 166).

Evangelism with such love—such pure motives and methods— as well as such intense conviction is God's objective for the church today. We see encouraging signs among us that God's church is returning to its apostolic beginnings in all these respects, especially in countries where the gospel has been suppressed until recently or is currently opposed with violence. The church is aglow with fresh vitality; its evangelism is generally untainted by doctrinal compromise, undimmed by false gifts or feigned love.

Reader, please do not feel left out of Christ's call to every-member participation in the finishing of His work, because He seeks to enlist you in His service. Follow Him, and He will make you a fisher of men (Matt. 4:19). The more you realize your natural insufficiency for this task, the more easily Christ can teach you how to labor effectively for Him (2 Cor. 3:3-6).

The gospel commission has not expired or been reduced in scope. We are still bidden to make disciples of all nations, baptizing them in the name of the Father, Son, and Holy Spirit, teaching them to observe all that Christ has commanded. And He who has all power in heaven and earth will be with us to the completion of this task (Matt. 28:18-20). Jesus promised to endow His disciples with the full outpouring of the Holy Spirit to accomplish this stupendous mission (Luke 24:49; Acts 1:8, 9). His promise not only is good for all probationary time, but is especially amplified in the closing days of His work for the world's salvation. The final outpouring of His Spirit shall completely cover the earth with a glorious revelation of His truth, His love, and His power to save (Joel 2:23-32; Rev. 18:1). He offers all His people the privilege of being instruments for the manifestation of that power (Rev. 22:17).

"He who called the fishermen of Galilee is still calling [men, women, and children] to His service. And He is just as willing to manifest His power through us as through the first disciples. However imperfect and sinful we may be, the Lord holds out to us the offer of partnership with Himself, of apprenticeship to Christ. He invites us to come under the divine instruction, that, uniting with Christ, we may work the works of God" *(The Desire of Ages*, p. 297).

Won't you respond to His recruitment call?

Lift Him Up

Lift Him up, 'tis He that bids you,
Let the dying look and live;
To all weary, thirsting sinners,
Living waters will He give;
And though once so meek and lowly,
Yet the Prince of heaven was He;
And the blind, who grope in darkness,
Through the blood of Christ shall see.

Lift Him up in all His glory,
'Tis the Son of God on high;
Lift Him up, His love shall draw them,
E'en the careless shall draw nigh;
Let them hear again the story
Of the cross, the death of shame;
And from tongue to tongue repeat it;
Mighty throngs shall bless His name.

Refrain:
Lift Him up, the risen Savior,
High amid the waiting throng;
Lift Him up, 'tis He that speaketh,
Now He bids you flee from wrong.

—May E. Warren

Peaceful Conquerors

5

Tongues of fire! A mighty, rushing wind! Untutored men exalting in many languages the resurrected Christ! What could it all mean?

Only 50 days earlier the very same speakers had dispersed from the upper room with fear at the arrest of their leader. Now their local adversaries and Jews of every nation were gathering to hear a message of indictment curiously mingled with offered pardon and hope.

On the day of Pentecost Jesus revealed Himself in power to the church through the Holy Spirit. The apostles were ready to receive the gift and be clear communicators of the outflow of Heaven's love to a world in spiritual drought. And thousands were converted in a day, with conversions continuing thereafter in a steady stream throughout the apostles' lives. That Pentecost of A.D. 31 was not an ephemeral feast, but the inauguration of an era of ceaseless evangelism, which nothing but the abandonment of first love could stop.

What qualified the apostles to bear such clear, courageous witness for their Saviour as that recorded in Acts 2? The answer is their heart-filled absorption with Jesus Christ and Him crucified, Him resurrected, Him interceding, and Him preparing a place in His kingdom for all who accept His salvation.

But just after Calvary the disciples were in no way prepared for this vast missionary enterprise. Jesus spent 40 days with them following His resurrection to help them prepare. During this time He did not introduce new teachings or manifest new powers, except to give them a preliminary endowment of the Holy Spirit (John 20:22). It was now His primary aim to anchor their minds and hearts to the power of His truth and grace as He had revealed it to them throughout their last three and a half years together. He outlined their work and clarified the message they were to deliver, showing them all these things from Scripture, especially the prophecies concerning Himself, to establish a sure, unshakable foundation for their faith (Luke 24:36-53; John 21:19-25).

Upon His ascension at the end of the 40 days and just 10 days prior to Pentecost, Jesus promised His disciples that they would be baptized with the Holy Spirit "not many days hence," reminding them that when they had the infilling of the Spirit it would then be their work to take the gospel to their own nation first and from there to the rest of the world (Acts 1:4-8).

Why was it so important for the apostles to receive the Holy Spirit? The reason for them is the same as it is for us—only through the Holy Spirit could they have a living relationship with Christ and be able to partake of His nature as well as receive His power for service and victorious Christian living (see John 14-16).

"The Holy Spirit is the breath of spiritual life in the soul. The impartation of the Spirit is the impartation of the life of Christ. It imbues the receiver with the attributes of Christ. Only those who are thus taught of God, those who possess the inward working of the Spirit, and in whose life the Christ-life is manifested, are to stand as representative men, to minister in behalf of the church" *(The Desire of Ages*, p. 805).

During those intense days of waiting just after Christ's ascension, the apostles prayed earnestly for the descent of the Holy Spirit, as Christ had told them to do. They put away differences from among themselves and continued in fellowship together, rejoicing in the power of Christ's truth and salvation. They prayed for a fitness to bring souls to the Saviour. They repented of their former stubbornness and hardness of heart that had so often made them misconstrue Christ's teaching and actions and to criticize one another. And above all, they meditated on Christ and contemplated His wonderful love, His mercy, His patience, His teachings, and His unselfish toil for the good of all. They longed to breathe His Spirit and bear His image so that they might serve Him acceptably in the continuation of His work. (Read *The Acts of the Apostles*, pp. 35-37.)

Their waiting and watching in such a spirit of humble devotion opened the way for an inflow of dynamic forces that encompassed the world. The Holy Spirit came upon the apostles with a power that had never before been witnessed through humanity. Multitudes were converted in a day, and the process continued unsubsiding for a long time afterward. This was not merely an emotional experience. New converts "continued stedfastly in the apostles' doctrine and fellowship and in breaking of bread, and in prayers" (Acts 2:42). The Lord added daily to the church all who accepted the gospel (verse 47).

Thus the early church went on "conquering, and to conquer" not in its own strength, but in the power of the Holy Spirit quickening hearts everywhere through the proclamation of the pure gospel (Col. 1:21-23; 1 Thess. 1:4-10; Rev. 6:2).

The secret of the apostles' power was that in them Christ's life was manifested, and they spoke for Him authoritatively, not deviating from sound doctrine and not misrepresenting the spirit of the word that they proclaimed (Rom. 6:17; Titus 2:7-10; 1 John 1:1-4). Such a solid regimen made for healthy converts. "The one who is feeble among them . . . shall be like David, and . . . like God, like the Angel of the Lord" (Zech. 12:8, NKJV). "Every Christian saw in his brother a revelation of divine love and benevolence. One interest prevailed; one subject of emulation swallowed up all others. The ambition of the believers was to reveal the likeness of Christ's character and to labor for the enlargement of His kingdom" *(The Acts of the Apostles*, p. 48). Their strength was not in superior intellect or will power, but in constant communion with Him.

Because of their complete absorption in Christ and the increase of His kingdom, He was free to expand all their faculties. They were enabled to do the deeds of omnipotence, not with boastful pride, but with humble yet courageous devotion to God's honor and with a quenchless love for everyone, including their worst opponents. The early believers regarded no sacrifice as too great, no call as too demanding, in response to the voice of Christ calling them onward, ever onward in extending the triumphs of the cross.

Their lives were an undivided investment in Him. Christ took no subordinate place in their affections. They recognized the truth that John Ruskin noted 19 centuries later: "He who offers God a second place offers Him no place." The devotion of these early believers was never meant to decline, but to increase with the progress of the gospel commission. The history of the early church is not just to command our admiration, but to inspire our own witness for the Lord.

After he was shot, President James Garfield was taken to a quiet, isolated house where he could have undisturbed quiet and rest. A special railway was constructed to facilitate bringing doctors, nurses, and family members to his bedside. The tracks as laid out had to cross through a farmer's front yard. Incensed when he saw the construction crew coming up to his place, he ordered them to leave. But when the engineers told him it was for the sake of the stricken president, the farmer's attitude changed immediately. He said, "Oh, if it's for President Garfield, I don't mind if you run the tracks straight through my house."

The Lord wants to run His tracks straight through your heart so that He can deliver the gospel news through you as by railway express. Give Him first place to do this, or His message through you is likely to end up in the dead letter office, even though you may achieve many other interesting things in life.

"All that the apostles did, every church member today is to do. And we are to work with as much more fervor, to be accompanied by the Holy Spirit in as much greater measure, as the increase of wickedness demands a much more decided call to repentance.

"Everyone on whom is shining the light of present truth is to be stirred with compassion for those who are in darkness. From all believers, light is to be reflected in clear, distinct rays. . . . At this time, when the end of all things is at hand, should not the zeal of the church exceed even that of the early church?" *(Testimonies,* vol. 7, p. 33). Zeal for what? Zeal to tell the story of redeeming love, of a crucified and risen Saviour; zeal to serve humanity as Christ did when He sojourned among us.

The early church members, animated by just such zeal, discovered that consecrated enthusiasm alone does not take the place of organized planning and action. They learned, in fact, that gospel labor and church organization are inseparably connected. The first major challenge facing the early church, which underscored the need for organization, was a controversy regarding equitable treatment for Greek widows who needed humanitarian assistance. The Greeks felt that the church favored Jewish widows above their own.

The ensuing strife gave rise to the appointment of seven deacons to help handle such affairs and thus leave the apostles free to pray, study, and preach (Acts 6).

"The appointment of the seven to take the oversight of special lines of work proved a great blessing to the church. These officers gave careful consideration to individual needs as well as to the general financial interests of the church, and by their prudent management and their godly example they were an important aid to their fellow officers in binding together the various interests of the church into a united whole" *(The Acts of the Apostles*, p. 89).

As a result of these steps in organization, a blessed unity prevailed among believers and a consistency of development as the church drew more and more people from diverse cultures into the ever-widening circle of its fellowship.

The extension of the gospel far and wide showed the need to establish churches and appoint officers to guide and train new converts and to perpetuate the work of the gospel and preserve its integrity. (See Acts 14:23; 16:4, 5; 1 Tim. 4:11-16; 2 Tim. 2:2; Titus 1:4-11.)

Another occasion arose that demonstrated the necessity of thorough organization and unity in the church. A major doctrinal controversy regarding the role of God's law threatened to split the church in two or perhaps tear it to fragments. Jewish Christians felt it incumbent on them to impose the obligations of the ceremonial law (such as circumcision) on Gentile converts. The matter was wisely settled in a general council of churches held at Jerusalem, which included representation from all Christendom. Emerging from this hot and potentially divisive controversy came a vigorous clarification of sound doctrine regarding the proper relationship between the ceremonial and moral laws. Thus, arising from contention and debate, greater and more intelligent unity was brought into the ranks of the church than had existed before. Without the Spirit's superintendence and the goodwill of the early believers this would not have been possible.

Guided by God's Word and the Holy Spirit, the apostles and elders "framed and issued [a] decree, which was thereupon generally accepted by the Christian churches" *(ibid.,* p. 196). "The broad and far-reaching decisions of the general council brought confidence into the ranks of Gentile believers, and the cause of God prospered" (*ibid.,* p. 197).

James presided at this general council of churches convened to deal with the intricate difficulty. It was largely the progressive work of Paul in advancing the cause of the gospel among the Gentiles and asserting little-understood truths regarding the proper relation of the law to the gospel that sparked the debate. Paul was a mighty champion of truth, and he demolished false, Pharisaic ideas that clung like rusty chains to the minds of many of the Jewish Christians, including to an extent even the other apostles.

No consideration of the apostolic church would be complete without a close study of the apostle Paul's work. In a book of this scope we have space to mention only some key points. After converting Saul the persecutor to Paul the Christian, Christ directed Ananias to connect His new disciple with the church. When Ananias demurred because of Saul's reputation as the fiercest of persecutors, Jesus said to him: "Go thy way: for he is a chosen vessel unto me, to bear my name before the Gentiles, and kings, and the children of Israel" (Acts 9:15).

Paul's role was rich and diverse. Preeminently he was a mighty clarifier of doctrine. With prophetic insight Paul dealt with complex controversies that would assail the church until the close of time. However, his might resided not only in his gigantic grasp of doctrinal issues, but also in his profound compassion, his thorough decency, and his unfailing courtesy in dealing even with the most difficult matters and people. His letters are permeated with a kindly, caring spirit that temper his sternest reproofs and most stirring exhortations.

Those who prayerfully and teachably read Paul's 14 epistles (we include Hebrews as among his writings, though some scholars question its Pauline origin) have the privilege of not only gaining a rich measure of his grasp of divine truth, but also becoming imbued with his courage, integrity, foresight, prudence, generosity, zeal, adaptability, balance, self-denial, and singleminded devotion to duty (Acts 20:17-37; 1 Cor. 7:19; 9:19-27; Eph. 3:1-10; Phil. 4:9; 1 Thess. 2:4-13). In Paul all these qualities were enveloped by a deep appreciation of Christ's cross (Gal. 2:20; 6:14; Phil. 2:1-12; 3:8-14). Through reading his words the same blessings are transmitted to us according to our faith and receptivity. That is why Paul could say under inspiration:

"Be ye followers of me, even as I also am of Christ" (1 Cor. 11:1). This is not to disparage the teachings and influence of the other apostles, but to note that more is revealed in Scripture about the inner workings of the apostolic mind through the life and sayings of Paul than through all his fellow apostles combined.

Paul's frailties are recorded too, lest we think his exalted spiritual experience altogether beyond our reach (e.g., Acts 15:37-39; 2 Cor. 12:7-12). But Paul learned quickly and was motivated to change for the better in order that God might be glorified in his life without misrepresentation or compromise. Throughout Paul's active life of service, Christ's love constrained him more and more in all that he said and did (2 Cor. 5:14). When this is also true with us, the primitive fire and fervor of the apostolic church will flare up in our church with unflagging incandescence and heat. And as at Pentecost the Holy Spirit will pass through our midst like a mighty rushing wind, driving us on to do and dare for our Lord and Saviour, Jesus Christ, until the whole earth is lightened with His glory!

Into All the World
His Grace and Glory

6

William Carey (1761-1834) seemed destined by his training and position in society to remain a shoemaker all his life. But after becoming converted to Christ in his youth, a flame of desire sprang up in his heart to evangelize the remote parts of earth where the gospel had not been heard for centuries. While he plied his trade at his small shop in Northampton, England, he would gaze at a large map of the world hung over his work desk and day by day prayerfully ponder the need of active missionary effort in such places as Africa, South America, and India.

Carey became a lay preacher in the Baptist Church, and went everywhere that he could get a hearing to promote the cause of missions, which in eighteenth-century England had little support and much scorn. Once while at a convention of ministers Carey made an appeal from the floor to evangelize unentered territory. A distinguished elder clergyman thundered with indignation, "Sit down, young man. When the Lord is ready to bring the gospel to the heathen, He will do so without your help or mine!" But others were moved by Carey's appeal, and eventually he found cautious sponsorship.

Though lacking a college education, he taught himself biblical and European languages. In the face of ecclesiastical and political opposition both in England and abroad, he established a college for the translation of Scripture. Carey mastered Sanskrit, Bengali, and several other Indian languages. In all he supervised the translation of the Bible into 40 Asian tongues.

Thanks to Carey and a few others like him, the work of mis-

47

sions was given a mighty forward push in the late eighteenth century, and this movement has been gaining momentum ever since.

Like Carey, we must realize that "the church . . . is God's appointed agency for the salvation of men. Its mission is to carry the gospel to the world. And the obligation rests upon all Christians. Everyone, to the extent of his talent and opportunity, is to fulfill the Saviour's commission. The love of Christ, revealed to us, makes us debtors to all who know Him not. God has given us light, not for ourselves alone, but to shed upon them.

"If the followers of Christ were awake to duty, there would be thousands where there is one today proclaiming the gospel" *(Steps to Christ*, p. 81).

It has been wisely said that "missions are the footsteps of the Almighty on His way to the final triumph of the gospel."

The gospel is everlasting. Since our first parents fell, God has desired to evangelize the world with a knowledge of the Saviour (Gen. 3:15; 1 Peter 1:18-20; Rev. 13:8). This revelation has been obscured not by faulty communication of God's part, but by a faulty response on humanity's part. Enoch, who walked with God, preached the gospel when this young world was already far advanced in wickedness (Jude 14, 15). God translated Enoch to heaven. Noah, too, was a preacher of righteousness (2 Peter 2:5). Although his contemporaries greeted Noah's message with jeering contempt, he faithfully labored on, mightily pleading with them to heed the merciful words of warning that he proclaimed for God.

Another evidence of God's loving interest in the world from its beginning is Jonah's commission to warn Nineveh of its impending destruction because of its cruelty and corruption. The Ninevites' short-lived repentance secured a reprieve. Meanwhile, they learned that YHWH, the God of Creation, had extended His mercy to them. Thus His character was revealed to a turbulent, warlike people who worshiped devils in the shape of brutal gods.

Untiringly the Holy Spirit ministered directly even to those societies which so withdrew themselves from God that they lost virtually all knowledge of His Word and will. God appealed to them by His moral influence and the ever-present messages of love communicated through nature (Gen. 6:3-9, 11-13; Rom. 1:19-21; 2:12-16; 2 Peter 3:9-15).

We may reasonably conclude, from the whole tenor of the Bible, that God gives each generation ample opportunity to decide for or against Him and holds people accountable only for light He has revealed (John 3:17-21; 2 Cor. 8:12). While the revelation of divine truth was not so full prior to the cross as it has been since (Matt. 13:16, 17; 1 Peter 1:9-12), Christ has always worked perseveringly to attract each person to Himself, the source of life, light, and salvation (John 1:9). He compassionately judges all in accordance with the light and opportunities He has extended to them (see Ps. 87:4-6; Acts 17:22-31). Throughout all history the entire nature of His dealings with human beings has been redemptive and evangelistic. His message rings down through the ages with resounding appeal and ever-mounting intensity: "Look unto me, and be ye saved, all the ends of the earth: for I am God, and there is none else" (Isa. 45:22).

Many more people than we can conceive of, from all ages and every part of the globe, have responded to this call. The redeemed, while not in the majority of earth's total population since Adam, shall be as innumerable as the sand on the seashore (Heb. 11:12; Rev. 7:9). Among these will be many who, though they never heard Christ's name, still heard His voice calling them into blessed association with Himself, into purity and love through the invisible work of His grace on their hearts. When Christ takes His royal bride, the church, to heaven, these will be part of that ennobled throng. With wonderment they shall ask about Him and then shall hear for the first time the heart-melting story of Christ's sacrifice. But during their earthly lives they had intuitively grasped His love and were transformed by it to receive His spiritual attributes.

The story is told of an African woman who learned how to read the Bible. A European missionary, observing her as she tearfully read the Gospel of Matthew, asked her how she felt about the story of Jesus. She said, "Oh, friend, I always knew that such a Saviour as this must have existed, but not until reading this book did I learn His name and the nature of His wonderful work for me."

The Lord's plan has always been to make Himself as openly and widely known as possible to the world He created and sustains. As we saw in chapter 2 of this book, He commissioned Abraham as a light bearer to the world and the forefather of Israel. God wanted

Israel to be the crown jewel of nations through which He would attract the world into a saving relationship with Himself. It was His plan to make Jerusalem the spiritual capital of earth, a city through which He would illuminate the world with the light of salvation (Ps. 48; 122; Isa. 62:1-7). The fascinating, instructive Temple services carried out there were meant to impart to the world a knowledge of Christ and His salvation. Moreover, God gave Israel equitable social laws—enlightened counsels on health, agriculture, and all the practical issues of life to maximize the personal and social happiness of His people (Deut. 4:6-9; Isa. 5:1-4; 12:2-6; 27:6). Israel's calling as a nation of kings and priests was to evangelize the world through exhibiting the beauty of holiness in Spirit-filled lives governed and inspired by His Word.

Their triumphs and failures as a people are recorded for our admonition, because the great gospel commission has passed from literal Israel to the church, God's spiritual New Jerusalem on earth. All the spiritual privileges and obligations that rested on ancient Israel are transferred to the church (Matt. 21:33-44; 23:37-39; 1 Peter 2:9). Illuminated with God's grace and glory, the church is the city that, set on Zion's hill, cannot be hidden (Matt. 5:14). The power and extent of her light is in proportion to her faithfulness in exemplifying God's Word (Eph. 5:8-17).

The gospel is not simply to ooze out of the church like sap from a tree to be collected by any willing seekers for truth; it is to burst forth like a fountain that irrigates the world. The church is not an information booth with passive personnel, but a telecommunications agency seeking to attract the world's attention to Christ and His salvation. A. J. Gordon said: "Though our task is not to bring all the world to Christ, our task is unquestionably to bring Christ to all the world" (in Walter B. Knight, *Master Book of New Illustrations*, p. 410).

Our enthusiasm to communicate the gospel to our neighbors and to regions beyond need not be artificially aroused. For "all who receive the gospel message into the heart will long to proclaim it. The heaven-born love of Christ must find expression. Those who have put on Christ will relate their experience, tracing step by step the leadings of the Holy Spirit—their hungering and thirsting for the knowledge of God and of Jesus Christ whom He has sent, the results of their searching of the Scriptures, their prayers, their soul agony, and the words of Christ to them, 'Thy sins be forgiven thee.' It is unnatural for any to keep these things secret, and those who are filled with the love of Christ will not do so. In proportion as the Lord has made them depositaries of sacred truth will be their desire that others shall receive the same blessing. And as they make known the rich treasures of God's grace, more and still more of the grace of Christ will be imparted to them" *(Christ's Object Lessons*, p. 125).

Those who love the Lord know the truth of this passage. Yet it is also true that many who love Jesus and would like to share their faith wish they had some instruction from people of experience. This is where the church can, or at least should, be of great help.

"Many would be willing to work if they were taught how to begin. They need to be instructed and encouraged. *Every church should be a training school for Christian workers.* Its members should be taught how to give Bible readings, how to conduct and teach Sabbath school classes, how best to help the poor and to care for the sick, how to work for the unconverted. There should be schools of health, cooking schools, and classes in various lines of Christian help work" *(Christian Service*, p. 59; italics supplied).

"The work of God in this earth can never be finished until the men and women comprising our church membership rally to the work, and unite their efforts with those of ministers and church officers" *(ibid.,* p. 68). But all need to know that they are welcome to do this. Church leaders should personally invite the members to assist them in gospel work.

One of my greatest joys as a pastor is to take church members with me in visitation and Bible studies. I feel that my work is seriously limited in value and purpose if I cannot share in this ministry with fellow believers. The pastor is not called to be a solitary reaper, but a trainer of gospel workers; the trainees are the congregation. Thanks to North American Division Evangelism Institute and the widespread efforts of the church leadership during the past two decades, the concept of the pastor as a teacher of the art and science of soul winning has increasingly taken root in North America. But this plan has been in healthy practice in Africa, Inter-America, South America, the Philippines, and other places for a much longer time. The church everywhere is awakening with new alertness to its mission.

Centuries ago a Christian philosopher said: "Kindle the dry sticks, and the green ones will catch." Come ablaze for Christ, and you will not have to spend one minute bemoaning the inactivity of others. Wholeheartedly launch into soul winning, and you'll be amazed at how many once-indifferent church members catch the vision that *every* member of the church is to be an active soul winner. True, some because of advanced age or illness may be able to do little more than pray, make phone calls, or write letters. But these ministries are not of minor value. Just to know that someone who loves the Lord is praying for souls you're trying to bring to Jesus will give immense lift to your spirits and will increase the effectiveness of your work. The Lord will answer His people's prayers for the salvation of others. Letters with a missionary purpose can also have incalculable value. In this age of television, video games, and thousands of useless diversions, letter writing has almost become a lost art.

I mention these ideas of quiet ministry to indicate the value of the often unrecognized efforts made for the Lord. Not all ministry comes into the general notice of the church or community, but the multitude of unsung services performed in faith are precious seed destined to bring forth a harvest of redeemed souls.

All who have willing hearts can do something useful for the Master. "Whether the amount [of talents] entrusted is large or small, the Lord requires that His householders do their best. It is not the amount entrusted or the improvement made [i.e., visible outcome] that brings to men the approbation of Heaven, but it is the faithfulness, the loyalty to God, the loving service rendered, that brings the divine benediction, 'Well done, good and faithful servant'" (*Our High Calling*, p. 289).

We must remember that counsel lest Satan tempt us, with all too frequent success, to do nothing for fear of failure or because we have been duped into believing that our "minor" efforts are of no consequence. One kindly word, one loving deed, can turn the tide of a discouraged or tempted person's life in the right direction for eternity.

A small but significant incident from history illustrates this point. A man who was traveling through a village in Northern Ireland heard the voices of children playing. Following the voices, he came to a small schoolhouse where the children were enjoying recess. One little boy stood apart from the rest, looking very sad.

The traveler asked the teacher, "Who is that boy?"

"Oh," said the teacher, "he amounts to nothing. He's the dullest boy in the school. I can't make him learn."

The visitor was grieved to hear the teacher speak so cruelly about the sad-faced child. Going up to the lonely lad, he spoke kindly to him.

A faint smile of hope flickered on the boy's face. And the stranger's parting words to him were "One of these days you'll make a fine scholar. Don't give up; try, my boy, try."

These words awakened the boy's sleeping mind. From that moment he resolved to fulfill the kind stranger's prophecy. That boy, Adam Clarke, became one of the most learned scholars of all time, whose commentary on the Bible is still highly prized more than a century and a half after it was first published.

If we perpetually sow words and deeds of kindness, they are sure to bear a bountiful harvest for the glory of God and the good of others. Jesus said: "As my Father hath sent me, even so send I you" (John 20:21). He goes forth with us to teach us how to be soul prospectors, and He gives us His Spirit to make our labors effective. He has ordained every true convert to bring forth lasting fruit for His kingdom (John 15:16; 2 Cor. 9:8-11).

Our great example of missionary activity is Jesus Himself. "[He] came to this world as the unwearied servant of man's necessity. . . . It was His mission to bring to men complete restoration; He came to give them health and peace and perfection of character. . . .

"The Saviour's work was not restricted to any time or place. His compassion knew no limit. . . .

"Christ came to this world to show that by receiving power from on high, man can live an unsullied life. With unwearying patience and sympathetic helpfulness He met men in their necessities. By the gentle touch of grace He banished from the soul unrest and doubt, changing enmity to love, and unbelief to confidence. . . .

"At the sound of His voice the spirit of greed and ambition fled from the heart, and men arose, emancipated, to follow the Saviour.

"Christ recognized no distinction of nationality or rank or creed. . . . He came to show that His gift of mercy and love is as unconfined as the air, the light, or the showers of rain that refresh the earth.

"The life of Christ established a religion in which there is no caste, a religion by which Jew and Gentile, free and bond, are linked in a common brotherhood, equal before God. No question of policy influenced His movements. He made no difference between neighbors and strangers, friends and enemies. That which appealed to His heart was a soul thirsting for the waters of life.

"He passed by no human being as worthless, but sought to apply the healing remedy to every soul" *(The Ministry of Healing*, pp. 17-25).

If we imbibe the spirit of Christ as described in this quotation, our lives will be a spiritual magnet drawing others to the Saviour. Our love for Him, for one another, and for all will preach a sermon that no sophistry or gainsaying can refute. A rose loses none of its fragrance for being called a thistle by its detractors. Christlike love, consistently exercised, has undeniable appeal whatever opposition it may face. Heaven's truth expressed with Heaven's kindness does not await popular acceptance to be convincing to honest minds.

In Isaiah 58:6-14 and Matthew 25:34-40, the Lord outlines the ministry of compassion in which He would have all His children engage. "It is only by an unselfish interest in those in need of help that we can give a practical demonstration of the truths of the gospel. . . . The union of Christlike work for the body and Christlike work for the soul is the true interpretation of the gospel" *(Welfare Ministry*, pp. 32, 33). "I cannot too strongly urge all our church members, all who are true missionaries, all who believe the third angel's message, . . . to consider the message of the fifty-eighth chapter of Isaiah. The work of beneficence enjoined in this chapter is the work that God requires His people to do at this time" *(Testimonies,* vol. 6, p. 265).

It is no casual connection that exists between Sabbathkeeping and the works of mercy mentioned in Isaiah 58. The two are integrally allied, because the Sabbath, with its freedom from ordinary labors that must be done for a living, provides every believer with enhanced opportunity to unselfishly serve others. Care for the sick, hungry, indigent, and brokenhearted is not, however, just a weekly or occasional work, but the daily task of all who love the Saviour. Care for the suffering and needy is not just a program—it's a principle of committed love whose service is constant and persevering.

David Livingstone was nicknamed "Sekeseke" by a certain tribe in Africa. In the language of that tribe a sekeseke is a small animal that can bore its way through any kind of wood or earthen structure. It perseveres for hours or days, if necessary, to accomplish its aim. The tenacity and toughness of this little animal reminded them of Livingstone's determination to carry the gospel through the most forbidding jungles and on to the most hostile tribes. He took souls alive for the kingdom of heaven not by his perseverance alone, but by his kindness, justice, generosity, and Christlike love. He labored to end the slave trade in Africa and to a fairly large extent succeeded.

The job of the church is to bring a final end to Satan's slave trade of taking people captive at his will and roping them to his chariot of cruel triumph. We should be as persevering and dauntless at setting others free through the power of Christ and His word as Livingstone was—and as largehearted in our concern for the welfare of all humanity. What we do now we must do quickly, because the hour is rapidly descending wherein no one can work for another's salvation (John 9:4).

The Whole Body Fitly Joined Together

7

A minister was discussing with a group of church workers methods of systematic labor in evangelism. One man in the audience stood up and said with great emphasis, "What we need, brother, isn't organization, but power!"

The minister replied, "Thank you for that thought. But let me ask you a question. I drove here tonight in a car. Which did I need more to make my trip possible, burning fuel or an engine?"

"Well," replied the objector, a little crestfallen, "I guess you needed both."

It is true that organization without the power of the Holy Spirit is at best mechanical and uninspiring, and at its worst it can be oppressive and dictatorial. But the misuse of something does not invalidate its use altogether. Church organization ideally is to reflect the order, harmony, beneficence, and wisdom that govern the life and activities of heaven. Thus, for organization to function according to heaven's laws, it is essential for those in leadership to have pure characters, just principles, and kindly manners.

Such were the qualities found in the leaders whom Moses selected to help administrate justice and order in Israel (Ex. 18:13-23; Deut. 1:9-18). Solomon said: "When the righteous are in authority, the people rejoice; but when a wicked man rules, the people groan" (Prov. 29:2, NKJV) and "That which maketh a man to be desired is his kindness" (Prov. 19:22, ASV).

All Christians, not just leaders in the church, should be kind and honest. And sometimes leaders are taught by the nobler example of those whom they are appointed to lead.

It is instructive to consider how organization of the Christian church began and who instituted it. Christ ordained 12 apostles to form the nucleus of the church. He endowed them with administrative talents that enabled them to establish churches which were to remain strongly united as part of the same familial organization. The apostles became truly effective in their work when they assimilated the spirit of Jesus in their relations with others. They did not dictate to fellow believers, and employed no coercion or carnal methods to bring souls to Christ. Peter enjoined elders to be examples to the flock and not conduct themselves as lords over God's heritage (1 Peter 5:3). Paul, that mighty champion of godly living and church unity, could declare with perfect honesty: "Not that we have dominion over your faith, but are fellow workers for your joy; for by faith you stand" (2 Cor. 1:24, NKJV). This spirit of Christlike purity and love, coupled with a deep commitment to unity, engendered a favorable climate for the early church's rapid expansion (1 Cor. 12:11-13, 25; 1 Thess. 2:3-13; 2 Tim. 2:24-26).

This brings us to the very heart of organization—Christ's prayer and provision for unity among believers (John 17). A perfect unity exists among the three persons of the Godhead—Father, Son, and Holy Spirit. Such unity among humans is a sublime miracle. It is the fruit of Christ's love working within and therefore is the most convincing evidence of the gospel's power and authenticity (John 13:34; 17:20-23). Unity in the Godhead is the example, inspiration, and sustaining source for unity among ourselves.

By nature people are competitive, self-promoting, prejudiced, impure, unforgiving, and bigoted (Gal. 5:19-21; Titus 3:3). Only a complete transformation of character can take away the fractious elements of our nature that obstruct unity. The unity for which Christ prayed and labored is not an operational expedient or a facade.

It is the fruit of every disciple's loving relationship with God and fellow believers. It is the unity of loving devotion to Christ and His truth. It is the unity of conscientious cooperation with the Holy Spirit for the promulgation of truth and the salvation of souls. It is the unity of mutual interest in the highest good and best happiness shared among believers, with all esteeming others better than themselves. It is the unity of congregational worship and service being carried out with genuine love for God and for one another. It is the unity of incorruptible allegiance to eternal truth in all its practical bearings. It is the unity of intimate fellowship with the Father, Son, and Holy Spirit, individually and corporately enjoyed by all believers who are being sanctified through the truth.

Carefully consider the following words: "The instruction given me by One of authority is that we are to learn to answer the prayer recorded in the seventeenth chapter of John. We are to make this prayer our first study. . . . My brethren and sisters, I ask you to heed these words and to bring to your study a calm, humble, contrite spirit, and the healthy energies of a mind under the control of God. Those who fail to learn the lessons contained in this prayer are in danger of making one-sided developments, which no future training will ever fully correct" *(Testimonies,* vol. 8, p. 239).

Dwight L. Moody, that outstanding soul winner of the past century, said: "There is one thing I have noticed as I have traveled in different countries; I never yet have known the Spirit of God to work where the Lord's people were divided. Unity is one thing that we must have if we are to have the Holy Spirit to work in our midst.

"If a church is divided, the members should immediately seek unity. Let the believers come together and get the difficulty out of the way. If the minister of a church cannot unite the people, if those that were dissatisfied will not fall in, it would be better for that minister to retire [i.e., depart]. . . . The Spirit of God does not work where there is division, and what we want today is the spirit of unity amongst God's children, so that the Lord can work" *(Moody Stories,* pp. 83, 84).

It has been my experience as a pastor that those who lightly regard unity and are readily inclined to scrap it for the sake of "truth" have argumentative spirits and unbalanced ideas of truth that are riddled with inaccuracies of perception and interpretation. They forget that Christ's call for unity is an integral part of His truth and not a dispensable option to be enjoyed when convenient. The rejecters of unity also tend to have an automatic distrust of leadership and church authority but a vast confidence in their own feelings and ideas. They tend to be antagonistic to the concept of organization, and seem to think it impossible for church administrators to be honest people or for the church to come into enlightened harmony on cardinal issues.

It doesn't give me pleasure to write these words; they are the painfully reluctant conclusion of one who has had more exposure to the spirit of disaffection than he cares to recollect. Without question, unity in error is unacceptable, but Christ is leading a people to "be perfectly joined together in the same mind and the same judgment" (1 Cor. 1:10). To be sure, this unity must be after God's order, and not after the devising of human beings (Rom. 15:5, 6; Eph. 4:1-6, 10-15). I have repeatedly seen believers of integrity and goodwill come into the unity of truth over disputed matters when pride and argumentation are laid aside in favor of God's Word. Unity is not impossible, and it is not invariably purchased at the cost of moral compromise, as some who are cynical and contentious seem to imply.

Unity in Christ is not uniformity, loss of individuality, or mindless adherence to a rigid corporate policy. It is harmony of thought, action, and feeling rooted and grounded in the eternal, self-validating righteousness of God's way. True unity among believers is not a compromise but a consequence of coming into accord with God's Word and Spirit. But unity does not come about in some casual, automatic way; we must cultivate it. Paul encouraged believers to *endeavor* "to keep the unity of the Spirit in the bond of peace" (Eph. 4:3). Without conscientious commitment to unity on our part, the devil will keep our churches in unending turmoil over divisive issues. We must reject his strategy and resolve to hold together in loving accord, fully committed to the truth as it is in Jesus, and not become sidetracked over disputable matters (Rom. 14:1).

Certain "defenders of the faith" sometimes take needlessly divisive action in the name of reform. While it is true that for the sake of unity needful discussion is sometimes suppressed and wrongs glossed over, it is a violation of Christ's high priestly will to attempt to settle these problems in a belligerent, contentious way.

When addressing even the most grievous wrongs, we must preserve a conciliatory spirit if we are to honor Christ's prayer for unity and have sincere hopes for a solution. No one understands better than Christ how impossible it is to achieve unity unless our hearts are first in harmony with Him and His Word. But one of

God's chief attributes is kindness and longsuffering, even in the face of grave wrongs.

Those who see the need for reform must cultivate these attributes if they are to have a constructively reformative influence. Even if the wrong seems to prevail for a period, the Lord will resolve these difficulties in His own time and way without our having to become combative in advocating the right.

We must cultivate patience and maintain the truth in both teaching and practice, without becoming dismayed, remembering that ultimately "we can do nothing against the truth, but for the truth" (2 Cor. 13:8, NKJV). This includes the promise that even unpopular truths will eventually be vindicated in full and shall be recognized and honored by the faithful, without our trying to steady the ark, when it is all in God's hands. We need not lose confidence in Christ's church or His management of it.

Ellen White relates: "As all the different members of the human system unite to form the body, and each performs its office in obedience to the intelligence that governs the whole, so the members of the church of Christ should be united in one symmetrical whole. If the world sees a perfect harmony existing in the church, it will be a powerful evidence to them in favor of the Christian religion. Dissensions, unhappy differences, and petty church trials dishonor our Redeemer. All these may be avoided, if self is surrendered to God, and the voice of the church is obeyed. Unbelief suggests that individual independence increases our importance, that it is weak to yield to the verdict of the church our ideas of what is right and proper; but to cherish such views and feelings will bring anarchy into the church and confusion to ourselves. . . . God has made His church a channel of light, and through it He communicates His purpose, and His will; and individual judgment should yield to the authority of the church" ("The Unity of the Church," *Bible Echo*, Sept. 1, 1888).

In all ages—and most especially in our time—many governments, businesses, and churches have grossly abused authority. Because of this as well as the natural unruliness of the human heart, many resent the existence of *all* authority. Some even in God's last-day church hold this feeling. It would be blindly unrealistic to deny that some members have suffered from the abuse of authority by misguided officeholders in the church. Such problems are as old as fallen human nature and were found in the early church. An example is Diotrephes, an arrogant bully who tried to dominate his local church (3 John 9, 10; cf. Acts 20:29).

Diotrephes' harshly autocratic spirit did not mean that the whole church was at fault or that no one in the church was worthy to hold a leading position. By contrast, for example, Demetrius was an exemplary leader of the church, meriting John's special commendation (3 John 12). But Diotrephes' bad example communicates a clear warning. In this age of rampant egotism, short tempers, and high stress, we must remember that "every thread of a spirit of domineering needs to be taken away" *(The Upward Look,* p. 289). Why? Because it is unlike Christ, who is meek and lowly in heart, and it is very hurtful, humiliating, and disheartening to be the victims of it. The church is to correct those who act in the spirit of Diotrephes. The spirit of lording will not find any place in heaven, whose King is not a dictator but a deliverer. Those who serve Him truly, while resolute and fearless in upholding principle, also reflect His kind, gentle, and gracious nature.

This highlights the issue of spiritual qualifications for holding church office. As we've already noted, no corporate work ever succeeds without direction and leadership from people who know how to lead. And no one can lead effectively without first knowing how to follow legitimate authority. The Holy Spirit has given gifts to the church so that it can be led in the right manner and direction.

These gifts are spiritual abilities found in every faithful member of Christ's body (1 Cor. 12:1-13). Among these gifts are administration and pastoring/teaching for the guidance and edification of the church (verses 28-31; Eph. 4:8-13). Love gives legitimacy and value to the gifts and to those who exercise them. Without love the gifts and their accompanying offices become vehicles for self-exaltation and strife in the church (1 Cor. 13).

This famous chapter on love is not an interlude in Paul's weighty theological analysis of gifts. It is at the base and summit of all his thinking on the subject. His essential point is that without the love of Jesus at work in the gifts, they are nothing more than glittering toys at best, and they can become weapons of evil. An example of this is the gift of tongues, which some of the Corinthians were using egotistically rather than to edify the church or help those outside it (1 Cor. 14). The gifts are not for show, but for service.

Likewise church office is not for prestige and power, but for self-abnegating service. Jesus taught: "Whosoever will be chief among you, let him be your servant" (Matt. 20:27). This is a definitive reversal of the world's way and of natural human inclination. That is why Christ so painstakingly taught this principle to His disciples, each of whom was seeking first place (Luke 9:46; 22:24).

This spirit of self-seeking caused much dissention and mutual distrust among them and left them dismally unprepared for Calvary, the supreme event that dislodges human pride and ambition. The absolute necessity for the crucifixion of human pride and ambition in God's service can hardly be overstressed. It was this lack of self-crucifixion that produced the Crusades, the Inquisition, Louis XIV's France, and the persecutions and injustices that have blighted the history of the church from the second century to our time, and that will culminate in the final persecution of the remnant by professed Christians who think they are doing God a service. And this same lack of self-crucifixion, lack of heart union with Christ, has caused authoritarianism in the church all too often throughout its history.

"Christ was establishing a kingdom on different principles. He called men, not to authority, but to service, the strong to bear the infirmities of the weak. Power, position, talent, education, placed their possessor under the greater obligation to serve his fellows. To even the lowliest of Christ's disciples it is said, 'All things are for your sakes.' 2 Cor. 4:15.

"'The Son of man came not to be ministered unto, but to minister, and to give His life a ransom for many.' Among His disciples Christ was in every sense a caretaker, a burden bearer. He shared their poverty, He practiced self-denial on their account, He went before them to smooth the more difficult places, and soon He would consummate His work on earth by laying down His life. The principle on which Christ acted is to actuate the members of His church which is His body. In the kingdom of Christ those are greatest who follow the example He has given, and act as shepherds of His flock.

"The words of Paul reveal the true dignity and honor of the Christian life: 'Though I be free from all men, yet have I made myself servant unto all,' 'not seeking mine own profit, but the profit of many, that they may be saved.' 1 Cor. 9:19; 10:33. . . .

"In Christ's kingdom there is no lordly oppression, no compulsion of manner" *(The Desire of Ages,* pp. 550, 551).

Spiritual authority in the church is not the royal right of titled office, but the natural result of submission to God and His call to serve in partnership with Him. Integrity, courage, vision, resilience, kindness, courtesy, temperance, resourcefulness, diligence, consecration, and doctrinal soundness are required of spiritual leaders (Joshua 1:6-9; 1 Cor. 4:1, 2; 2 Cor. 6:4-10; 1 Tim. 3:1-6). Their primary task is to help church members discover and effectively utilize their spiritual gifts to advance the interests of God's kingdom (1 Cor. 1:4-9; Eph. 4:15, 16; 2 Tim. 2:2). Church leaders are also guardians of the flock with respect to the soundness of its message, mission, and membership.

This last named responsibility leads us into the very sensitive issue of church discipline. The idea of church discipline comes directly from Christ's instructions to the fledgling church: "If your brother sins against you, go and tell him his fault between you and him alone. If he hears you, you have gained your brother. But if he will not hear you, take with you one or two more, that 'by the mouth of two or three witnesses every word may be established.' And if he refuses to hear them, tell it to the church. But if he refuses even to hear the church, let him be to you like a heathen or a tax collector. Assuredly, I say to you, whatever you bind on earth will be bound in heaven, and whatever you loose on earth will be loosed in heaven" (Matt. 18:15-18).

"In the spirit of meekness, 'considering thyself, lest thou also be tempted' (Gal. 6:1), go to the erring one, and 'tell him his fault between thee and him alone.' Do not put him to shame by exposing his fault to others, nor bring dishonor upon Christ by making public the sin or error of one who bears His name. Often the truth must be plainly spoken to the erring; he must be led to see his error, that he may reform. But you are not to judge or condemn. Make no attempt at self-justification. Let all your effort be for his recovery. In treating the wounds of the soul, there is need of the most delicate touch, the finest sensibility. Only the love that flows from the Suffering One of Calvary can avail here. With pitying tenderness let brother deal with brother, knowing that if you succeed, you will 'save a soul from death' and 'hide a multitude of sins.' James 5:20" *(ibid.,* p. 440).

But if all efforts made in harmony with Christ's counsel in Matthew 18:15-17 prove unavailing and the cause is just, then the church has the solemn obligation to acknowledge formally the erring one's voluntary separation from fellowship with Christ, because only those who keep His Word truly love Jesus and honor the privilege of being part of His body (Luke 6:46; John 14:21-24).

Regrettably, sometimes the church's best efforts to restore an offender prove fruitless. Then "he who rejects this united overture has broken the tie that binds him to Christ, and thus has severed himself from the fellowship of the church. Henceforth, said Jesus, 'let him be unto thee as an heathen man and a publican.' But he is not to be regarded as cut off from the mercy of God. Let him not be despised or neglected by his former brethren, but be treated with tenderness and compassion, as one of the lost sheep that Christ is still seeking to bring to His fold" *(ibid.,* p. 441; see also pp. 805, 806).

Redemption, restoration, and preservation are the key purposes of all valid church discipline.

"The very snuffers of the tabernacle were made with pure gold, to show the purity of those censures, whereby the light of the church is kept bright. That power that is given to the church is given for edification, not destruction. How careful was St. Paul, that the incestuous Corinthian, 2 Cor. 2:7, repenting, should not be swallowed up with too much grief" *(The Works of Richard Sibbes,* p. 55).

But when the church administers appropriate discipline, it does no good to extend false sympathy to the offender, treating him or her as one who has suffered injustice at the hands of the membership. When an erring member is corrected by the church, he or she should receive the counsel with appreciation and not with sullen reluctance. "There are many who, when they are reproved, think it praiseworthy if they receive the rebuke without becoming impatient; but how few take reproof with gratitude of heart and bless those who seek to save them from pursuing an evil course" *(Patriarchs and Prophets,* p. 667). David prayed: "Let a righteous man strike me—it is a kindness; let him rebuke me—it is oil on my head. My head will not refuse it" (Ps. 141:5, NIV).

Although censure or disfellowshipment should be the last resort, after all other redemptive measures have been diligently tried, such discipline is not cruel or condemnatory if conducted in a Christlike manner. Paul when he censured the Corinthians and Galatians was not their enemy for telling them the truth, but their best friend (2 Cor. 7:7-12; Gal. 4:16). He cared enough for their salvation to warn them of their danger in departing from God's standards. "He who rebukes a man will find more favor afterward than he who flatters with the tongue" (Prov. 28:23, NKJV). God has committed to us a ministry of reconciliation, not of condemnation, yet that ministry includes reproof to the erring and encouragement to obey God's Word (2 Tim. 4:1, 2).

It is passive cruelty to offer no counsel or warning to fellow Christians who are wronging their own souls and hurting others, thereby dishonoring Christ. "It is not Christ's follower that, with averted eyes, turns from the erring, leaving them unhindered to pursue their downward course" *(The Desire of Ages*, p. 462).

But we are in no position to offer corrective counsel or administer discipline unless we are first willing to lay down our lives for the person we wish to help. This is the character of true love (1 John 3:16). Anything that falls short of this is likely to work more harm than good. Further, we must also be willing to have our own faults corrected (Matt. 7:1-5).

These clumsy feet, still in the mire,
Go crushing blossoms without end;
These hard, well-meaning hands we thrust
Among the heartstrings of a friend.

The ill-timed truth we might have kept—
Who knows how sharp it pierced and stung?
The word we had not sense to say—
Who knows how grandly it had rung?
—E. R. Sill

Some key points to observe in church discipline are:
1. Closely follow the counsel of Matthew 18:15-18.
2. Be prayerful, compassionate, loving, redemptive (Gal. 6:1, 2).

3. Examine your own heart for faults (Matt. 7:1-5).

4. Do not gossip about the problems you are seeking to correct (Lev. 19:16; Prov. 20:20-26).

5. Do not be vindictive, unforgiving, or condemnatory (2 Cor. 2:4-11).

6. Do not be self-righteous (Luke 18:9-14).

7. Do not allow open sin to go unreproved or unchecked (1 Cor. 1:10-14; 5; Gal. 2:11-14; 3 John 9-11).

8. Be ready to restore repentant wrongdoers to renewed confidence and fellowship (2 Cor. 7:8-12).

9. Do not cease to make kindly efforts to win back erring members who have strayed from the church (Mark 16:6, 7; 1 Thess. 5:14, 15; 2 Thess. 3:14, 15).

Christ's objective is to complete His family and take it to heaven without losing anyone who truly wants to be there. Every aspect of church organization is, under God's direction, designed to make the church an unbroken draw net by which to gather in souls for His kingdom. Breaches in the net mean lost souls! A church that is organized after heaven's beneficent order is a refuge of safety, righteousness, and redemption. The church is not only Christ's fortress; it is His family, and caring members of the family will sacredly guard the best interests of its individual members as well as of the corporate whole.

The Wonderful Numberer

8

One day in the late 1700s Rowland Hill was preaching to an outdoor audience in London. An eminent lady of the day, Anne Erskine, was driving by in her carriage. She asked her coachman, "Who is that speaker who holds his audience so rapt?"

He replied, "It's Rowland Hill, m'lady."

She said, "Drive closer to him; I've been wanting to hear that man."

The crowd made way for the carriage bearing the royal insignia on its door. Hill asked a bystander who the noble lady was. Upon being told, he shouted, "Stop, my friends! I have got something to sell." Taking up the role of an auctioneer, he spoke rapidly: "I have more than a title to sell. I have more than a crown of Europe to sell. It is the soul of Lady Anne Erskine. Will anyone here bid for it? Yes, I hear a bid. Satan, Satan, what will you give? 'I will give pleasure, honor, riches—yea, I will give the whole world for her soul.' Do I hear another bid? Is there no other? Yes, I hear another bid! It's from the Lord Jesus Christ. Jesus, what will you give for this soul? 'I will give peace, joy, comfort, that the world knows not of—yea, I will give eternal life in exchange for her heart.'"

Then looking straight through the coach window and fixing his eyes kindly on hers, Hill said slowly, "Lady Anne Erskine, you have heard the two bidders for your soul. Which will you accept?"

The royal lady, opening the door of her coach, came forth weeping and openly accepted Jesus Christ as her Saviour.

When we step forward unashamedly for Christ the way Anne

Erskine did, He conducts us into His banqueting house, where His banner over us is love, and there He inducts us into the fellowship of His people, who now become our people. We joyfully unite with them as fellow believers and joint heirs with Christ (S. of Sol. 2:1-3; Rom. 8:17).

Like marriage without love, church membership without a connection to Christ is irksome and valueless. But membership with a living connection to Christ is like a marriage in which love flourishes and feeds the relationship with continual freshness, creativity, and delight. Jesus taught His disciples the necessity of abiding in Him, and pointed out the rich privileges of that relationship—their Spirit-moved prayers are answered; they bring forth lasting fruit for His kingdom; they are cleansed and constantly grow in capacity to glorify God (John 15:1-16). Their lives are fulfilling instead of frustrating. They mature instead of regress. They are productive instead of barren. And they experience all these developments in fellowship with God and other believers.

Loving sociability in a spirit of service is the essence of heaven's life, and it is the fragrant atmosphere of the church's life. It all comes from a heart union with Christ. "Those who are accounted by God as His children will reveal Christlike love for one another. They will love and work for one object—the proper representation of Christ to the world. By their love and unity they will show to the world that they bear the divine credentials. . . .

"The most powerful evidence a man can give that he has been born again and is a new man in Christ Jesus is the manifestation of love for his brethren, the doing of Christlike deeds. This is the most wonderful witness that can be borne in favor of Christianity, and will win souls to the truth. . . .

"Christ brings all true believers into complete oneness with Himself, even the oneness which exists between Him and His Father. The true children of God are bound up with one another and with their Saviour. They are one with Christ in God" *(Sons and Daughters of God,* p. 293).

These fundamental truths are embodied in Christ's prayer in John 17, which we have already examined. The oneness of believers with Christ and with each other discloses a fascinating paradox. Christ accentuates the individuality of all who are one with Him; at the same time He brings the vividly unique individuality of all believers into rich, melodious harmony. The assembly of saints who truly love the Lord may be compared to an orchestra playing a symphony with a great variety of instruments, all combining in richly interwoven harmonies and subtly textured counterpoint. No instrument is identical in shape, timbre, or part played, but all the instruments, following the same score, sound as one, and all of them in combination sound better than any one of them playing alone. But when solos are played, they are enhanced by their connection with the orchestra. The analogy, of course, is limited because every orchestra has groups of the same instruments and some of the instruments at times play in unison, yet even then all performers impart a different accent to the instruments they play. This gives each instrumental section and every orchestra its distinctive character.

So the Holy Spirit orchestrates the church to be a choir of praise, as it were, to God (1 Cor. 12:4-7, 11; Eph. 1:5-13). Through the sounding forth of the gospel to the world, many join God's family. Thus the choir is enlarged, and His praises are increased in volume, variety, and intensity, while harmony is preserved intact. When discords do arise (from theological debate, perplexity arising over cultural differences, interpersonal clashes, etc.), the Holy Spirit teaches the choir how to achieve a richer harmony, a more inclusive melody, without violating or muting a single note of truth or a single feature of righteousness. This is the genius of God and His everlasting gospel, which brings forth gladness and singleness of heart in His ever-growing family (Acts 2:46; Eph. 2:10-14). Ultimately the whole choir, composed of converts from every nation, kindred, tongue, and people, will unitedly sing the praises of God in heaven, without a single discord or faltering note (Rev. 7:9, 10).

The Lord delights to add daily to His church such as should be saved (Acts 2:47). What does it mean to become a member of God's church? What privileges and responsibilities are linked with church membership? As mentioned before, church membership adds us to God's household. This is no nominal honor, but a real inclusion into a literal family whose bonds are not genetic but spiritual through fellowship with Christ.

The Lord is preparing His bride for His heavenly kingdom! That bride consists of His saved people, who will be living together as friends, neighbors, brothers, and sisters through all eternity. His church is the nursery for that eternal fellowship. He constantly seeks to make "increase of the body unto the edifying of itself in love" (Eph. 4:16). Does this mean that God is "numbers-oriented"? Yes, very much so! He is *palmoni*, the wonderful numberer (Dan. 8:13, margin), who numbers His sheep and keenly notices the absence of one and rejoices with all heaven over the addition of one more rescued sheep to His flock (Matt. 15:1-7). He is extending probationary time to add to the numbers of ransomed souls who shall enter His kingdom (John 10:16). Not willing that any should perish, He strives to bring every lost soul to repentance. No one in the universe is more concerned about "numbers" than Jesus Christ. Every person is infinitely precious in His sight, and you are one of that number. Moreover, Jesus wants you to so value every person, that through you He might accomplish their salvation.

His message to Israel should govern our philosophy of evangelism and nurture: "Enlarge the place of thy tent, and let them stretch forth the curtains of thy habitations: spare not, lengthen thy cords, and strengthen thy stakes; for thou shalt break forth on the right hand and on the left; and thy seed shall inherit the Gentiles, and make the desolate cities to be inhabited" (Isa. 54:2, 3).

One classic commentary says of this text: "Thy children shall be so many that thy borders must be extended to contain them. . . . [Therefore] give abundantly the means for the enlargement of the Church. . . . The Church is not merely to seek new converts, but to strengthen those she has in the faith" (Robert Jamieson, A. R. Fausset, and David Brown, *Commentary on the Whole Bible,* p. 492).

A blend of evangelistic zeal and loving nurture should characterize every church that calls itself Christian. Those congregations that are blessed with this vision grow spiritually and numerically without inordinate strain.

God adds members to the church through baptism (Mark 16:16; Acts 2:37-41). "Christ has made baptism the sign of entrance to His spiritual kingdom. He has made this a positive condition with which all must comply who wish to be acknowledged as under the authority of the Father, the Son, and the Holy Spirit. Before man can find a home in the church, before passing the threshold of God's spiritual kingdom, he is to receive the impress of the divine nature, *'The Lord our Righteousness.'* Jeremiah 23:6" *(Testimonies,* vol. 6, p. 91).

Baptism symbolically portrays the believer's death to self, burial of the old sinful past, and a rising up in newness of life in Christ through His gospel (Rom. 6:1-4; Col. 2:11-13). Christian baptism calls for repentance of sin and the acceptance of Christ's forgiveness and cleansing merits. Without that experience baptism is meaningless. Water baptism is of value only to those who have first been born of the Spirit (John 3:3-8). John refused to baptize unconverted people. Under the Spirit's anointing he saw through the hypocrisy of those who came to be baptized for self-serving reasons, and exhorted them to first bring forth the fruits of repentance in their lives (Matt. 3:7, 8). Baptism is not for those who are living in deliberate sin, but for those who have made a wholehearted commitment to Christ as Lord and Saviour of their lives (1 Peter 3:21).

"It is the grace of Christ that gives life to the soul. Apart from Christ, baptism, like any other service, is a worthless form" *(The Desire of Ages,* p. 181). The Spirit labors to bring forth conversion in every soul, and He will succeed with all who do not stubbornly fight Him off and thus commit the sin against the Holy Spirit (Gen. 6:3; Mark 3:29; Rom. 8:26; Gal. 5:16, 17). The truly born-again person will cooperate with the Spirit's work in the heart to put to death the sinful nature and its activities (Rom. 8:1-14).

Too often, I fear, we administer baptism prematurely, and thus give newly added church members a false sense of security, as well as a weak concept of what God has in mind for their Christian lives. Thus we unwittingly teach them to have lowered expectations of what divine grace is to accomplish in their hearts. "Baptism is a most solemn renunciation of the world. Those who are baptized in the threefold name of the Father, the Son, and the Holy Spirit, at the very entrance of their Christian life declare publicly that they have forsaken the service of Satan and have become members of the royal family, children of the heavenly King. They have obeyed the command: 'Come out from among them, and be ye separate, . . . and touch not the unclean thing.' And to them is fulfilled the promise: 'I will receive you, and will be a Father unto you, and ye shall be my sons and daughters, saith the Lord Almighty.' 2 Corinthians 6:17, 18.

"There is need of a more thorough preparation on the part of candidates for baptism. They are in need of more faithful instruction than has usually been given them. The principles of the Christian life should be made plain to those who have newly come to the truth. None can depend upon their profession of faith as proof that they have a saving connection with Christ. We are not only to say, 'I believe,' but to practice the truth. It is by conformity to the will of God in our words, our deportment, our character, that we prove our connection with Him" *(Testimonies,* vol. 6, pp. 91, 92).

Baptism seals our connection not only with Christ but also with His church (see Gal. 3:27; 1 Cor. 12:13). It is unscriptural to think of being baptized into Christ alone without belonging to any church, for to be baptized into Christ is inseparably to be baptized also into His body, the church. He has made no arrangements for His followers to embark upon a path of solitary discipleship. "None of us lives to himself alone, and none of us dies to himself alone" (Rom. 14:7, NIV). Christ desires to bring us into familial association with all Heaven and with all fellow believers on earth. He brings us near to Himself and to one another through the blood of His cross (Col. 1:20; Eph. 2:13-22).

To help cement His followers' connection with Him and with one another, Christ instituted another ordinance for the Christian church, the Lord's Supper. This service is to be preceded by washing one another's feet. John 13:1-17 tells the story of how Jesus, on the night before Calvary, instituted this service and established it as a permanent ordinance for the church. As you read the account, it is helpful to keep in mind that everything Jesus did that night was governed by His unwavering love for His disciples. This love, of course, applies to all humanity at all times, but only those who are in close relationship with Christ would see any value in His ordinances and be capable of discerning the glorious gospel lessons they symbolically portray. Always having our immediate and eternal interests in mind, He is ever mindful of His covenant, which is ordered in all things and sure. As you study this subject, probe for its deeper applications to your life; the meaning is simple, yet inexhaustible.

At the last Passover Christ was to enjoy with His disciples, He plainly saw the stony-hearted pride that kept each disciple from acting the part of a servant to wash the others' feet. Each was too intent on establishing his own supremacy, or at least maintaining a dignity that would exempt him from having to serve the others. This caused unbearable tension between them. Pride, jealousy, and evil surmising poisoned their fellowship, making that church service in the upper room sheer agony. Jesus saw it all. How could He purge them of this spirit of self-exaltation that froze the fountain of love in their hearts, making them foes instead of friends? Rather than rebuke or lecture them, He took a towel and washed their feet in a basin of water.

All this epitomized Christ's way of handling human weakness and pride. Always intrepid for truth and the honor of God, He was never self-assertive, never bent on establishing His own rights. His whole aim was to set sinners free from bondage to Satan. And Satan's strongest bond in the hearts of the disciples was pride. Christ's humble, self-effacing act of washing their feet broke the fierce bonds of pride in each disciple's heart, except Judas. Christ's humility confirmed Judas' resolve to disassociate from a program that called for self-denial, self-sacrifice, and loving service. He went out to betray Jesus. The lessons of that night carry through to the close of time.

"The ordinance of feet washing is an ordinance of service. This is the lesson the Lord would have all learn and practice. When this ordinance is rightly celebrated, the children of God are brought into holy relationship with each other, to help and bless each other.

"That His people might not be misled by the selfishness which dwells in the natural heart, and which strengthens by self-serving, Christ Himself set us an example of humility. He would not leave this great subject in man's charge. Of so much consequence did He regard it that He Himself, One equal with God, washed the feet of His disciples" *(The SDA Bible Commentary,* Ellen G. White Comments, vol. 5, pp. 1138, 1139).

No biblically logical reason exists for this ordinance not to continue throughout the New Testament dispensation. Jesus plainly said: "If I then, your Lord and Teacher, have washed your feet, you also ought to wash one another's feet. For I have given you an example, that you should do as I have done to you. . . . If you know these things, happy are you if you do them" (John 13:14-17, NKJV). Jesus further taught His disciples to teach others to observe all that He had commanded them to do (see Matt. 28:20).

Those who are receptive to the spirit of loving service taught in the ordinance of humility are then prepared for the Lord's Supper. This sublimely simple and beautiful celebration symbolizes Jesus' desire to become incorporated into our lives (John 6:48-63). The unleavened bread and unfermented wine typify His broken body and shed blood in sacrifice for our redemption (Luke 22:14-20). He wants us to appropriate the power of His new covenant, the saving merits of His atoning death for the sins of the world. Each Communion service educates us to look back to Calvary with thankful reverence, and forward to Christ's second coming, when He shall take us to His kingdom to partake with us of heaven's bread and grape juice (Matt. 26:29; 1 Cor. 11:26).

This service also educates us to be more vividly mindful of our Saviour here and now. We perform this service *in remembrance of Him* (1 Cor. 11:25). He wishes us to keep this New Testament Passover feast with sincere, heartfelt devotion and an eye single to His glory (1 Cor. 5:7, 8; 10:16, 17).

"The table in the upper room at Jerusalem was but a type and earnest of the table in the upper room of glory. Soon we shall exchange the table below for the table above, where we shall give full expression to our love for all eternity. There no betrayers can come—'no unclean thing can enter.' Jesus shall be at the head of the table, and God shall wipe away all tears from our eyes" *(Messages and Miscellaneous Papers of Robert McCheyne*, vol. 2, p. 239).

Some have wondered whether Christians today are bound to keep the ceremonial feasts of ancient Israel, because each of those feasts was emblematically saturated with gospel teaching. God's Word clearly answers that concern. The laws pertaining to the Hebrew sanctuary were ceremonial and remained in effect only until Calvary. When Jesus died, He brought to an end the system of animal sacrifices and sanctuary rituals, as the prophet Daniel predicted He would do (Dan. 9:27; cf. Matt. 27:50, 51; John 19:30).

This fact is enlarged upon by the apostle Paul (see, for example, Col. 2:13-17; Eph. 2:13-17; Heb. 8-10). Yet Paul was equally forceful in defending the perpetuity of God's moral law, drawing a careful distinction between it and the ceremonial ordinances (Rom. 3:31; 8:4; 13:8-10; Gal. 6:15; 1 Cor. 7:19; 9:21). Our attention is now directed to the sanctuary *above,* where Jesus intercedes for us to bring Calvary to life in our hearts.

The shadows of ceremonialism are forever dispelled in the golden gleams of Calvary love. And the church of God, reverently gathering around the cross, is baptized in its blazing light of eternal grace—baptized in the Spirit to go forth to a dark world and shed abroad the marvelous light of Christ's glorious gospel.

In the cross of Christ I glory,
Towering o'er the wrecks of time;
All the light of sacred story
Gathers round its head sublime.

Bane and blessing, pain and pleasure,
By the cross are sanctified;
Peace is there that knows no measure,
Joys that through all time abide.
—John Bowring

Called With
a Holy Calling

9

Selina was a bright and beautiful 9-year-old girl. A delightful playmate, she was always full of high spirits and interesting ideas. Her family was rich, happy, and popular. Then a shadow crossed Selina's path, a shadow that was destined to change the whole course of her life. While she was playing with her friends, a funeral procession approached. The girls stopped their play and asked one of the band of mourners, "Who has died?"

The answer was "A little girl."

"A little girl!" cried Selina, "Who was she?"

When told the child's name, Selina did not recognize it. The girl was a stranger to her but still was another child, like she was.

Selina asked, "How old was she?"

"Nine." Selina's age!

Breaking away from her playmates, Selina joined the cortege on its sad march to the graveyard on a hill several hundred feet away. After the casket was covered and the funeral party dispersed, Selina remained and wept over the grave. For the first time she was brought face-to-face with the solemnities of life and death. Henceforth she could no longer be a child of time, but of eternity!

Yet she could find no peace. She was a good child as far as behavior was concerned, but was distressed by her inner emptiness and coldness, her lack of deep love. Throughout her remaining childhood she prayed, read the Bible, and often wept for her sins and dullness of heart. But she could find no peace, no release. She went to church, but the services were frigid and formal, destitute of heavenly light or cheering hope.

Selina married well. Of royal lineage herself, she became a countess through uniting with the wealthy, powerful Earl of Huntington, a man of high principle in an age when this could be said of few titled persons.

The young Lady Huntington, wanting to please God, devoted herself to charitable services. Many of the poor, who in that age had little public assistance, benefited from Lady Huntington's generosity. Her life was morally irreproachable; balls, banquets, card parties, court intrigues, and the frivolous round of activities that characterized life among eighteenth-century aristocrats held no attractions for her. While her peers were at tea parties for gossip and gaiety, Lady Huntington read her Bible and sought wholesome companions and constructive duties. But still her heart felt empty and dry, because charitable deeds and upright conduct, though commendable, are not the pathway to redemption. Despondency crept over her soul like a deep chill. She took to her bed and slowly wasted away from the medically untreatable disease called despair.

As Lady Huntington's condition worsened during the following months, it was expected that she would soon die. Then her sister-in-law, Margaret Hastings, came to visit her. Margaret was all aglow with a newfound experience in the love of Christ. She had recently learned the way of salvation through listening to a Methodist field preacher. Margaret's testimony was: "Since I have trusted in the Lord Jesus Christ for life and salvation, I have been as happy as an angel!"

The words burned into Lady Huntington's soul. She thought more and more about what it meant to trust exclusively to the merits of a crucified and risen Saviour. Soon afterward, as she read one of her favorite portions of Scripture—the early chapters of 1 Corinthians—the text *"Other foundation can no man lay than that is laid, which is Jesus Christ"* (1 Cor. 3:11) blazed into life within her soul. She gave her heart to Christ not as some formal transaction, but in an abandonment of devotion and love. She soon recovered from her illness and was once more up and doing for her Master. Not now as a weary, wistful seeker of merit, but as a thankful servant and friend of her Lord and Saviour Jesus. She had found joy and peace in believing.

Lady Huntington became acquainted with Whitefield, the Wesleys, and scores of truly converted revivalists of her era. Devoting her enormous wealth to the furtherance of the gospel, she built Bible schools, churches, and chapels all across the British Isles and provided for many faithful ministers whom the state church refused to acknowledge. She also continued her bountiful care for widows, orphans, prisoners, and disabled people. But never did she suppose that her altruistic deeds constituted the ground or even the supplement of her future hopes. All her acts of kindness (which she thought little of herself) were simply the superstructure that she built upon the sure foundation of Christ and His righteousness. As her long life progressed, she lived more and more frugally, giving up all luxuries, including her jewels, so that she could provide for the extension of the gospel not only throughout her native England, but to foreign lands as well.

Just a few months before she died at the age of 84, Lady Huntington wrote: "I do hereby declare that all my present peace and my hope of future glory depend wholly, fully, and finally upon the merits of Jesus Christ, my Lord and Saviour. I commit my soul into His arms unreservedly as a subject of His sole mercy to all eternity." Only days before her death she stated in a voice ringing with conviction, "There is but one Foundation on which a sinner like me can rest: Jesus Christ, my Lord."

Never did so decent a person place less confidence in her decency, and comparatively few believers have made so full a commitment to serve God and extend the gospel as did she. But this is the reasonable service that Christ wishes to inspire in every child of His. Few Christians have had the material wealth that Lady Huntington possessed, but many have had the strength and longevity she enjoyed. It is the privilege of all believers to serve Jesus wholeheartedly in a spirit of grateful love for His unceasing service to us. That's the purpose of every practical aspect of Christian life. None of it is to earn favor with God or improve our chances for heaven. If heaven is in our hearts, so will the flowing spirit of its unselfish service be there, free from any vain thoughts of honor, reward, or preferment. Like Lady Huntington, we will devote our lives to building up God's kingdom on earth, and like her we will be active members of God's church. We will hunger to be a blessing to others and to unite with God's people in service and praise.

One of the richest privileges of Christian life and church membership is that of attending Sabbath services. Jesus' own observance of the Sabbath and His customary attendance of public worship set the example for us as Christians (Luke 4:16). The Sabbath, devoted to God's service, is a delight (Isa. 58:13, 14). Those who truly love the Lord will yearn for fellowship with Him and with others who love Him (1 John 1:7). Knowing how much the world would absorb and deplete the energies of His professed people in the last days, God exhorts us not to forsake the assembling of ourselves together, especially as we approach the end of time (Heb. 10:25; Rev. 3:14-17). The Lord designated the Sabbath as a time of holy convocation for His people; moreover He inseparably links His Sabbath and His sanctuary (Lev. 23:3; 26:2).

The purposes and blessings of church services are manifold. Church is preeminently a place of prayer. The believing women at Philippi, though they had no house of worship, customarily gathered by a riverbank to pray each Sabbath (Acts 16:13). God called His temple a house of prayer for all people (Isa. 56:7). When Solomon dedicated the Temple at Jerusalem, he pleaded with God to hear the petitions of Gentiles who visited the Temple to pray for His blessing (2 Chron. 6:32, 33). Through receiving God's gracious answers, Gentiles would thereby recognize His infinite mercy and power to bless and direct all human lives. Church is a refuge for weary souls longing for heaven's touch and the sound of Christ's voice speaking to their hearts (Ps. 84:1-4, 10). Its blessings are open to all who seek to know the Saviour.

Church is a house of sacrifice (2 Chron. 7:12). As we noted in the previous chapter, Christ's death on Calvary ended the system of animal sacrifices that God had anciently instituted to point people to the Lamb of God, who takes away the sin of the world. The sacrifices of a Christian are prayer, thanksgiving and praise, confession to God, and loving deeds—spiritual sacrifices that honor Him (Ps. 116:17; Isa. 51:16, 17; Heb. 13:15, 16; 1 Peter 2:5).

Church is a place for reading, preaching, and studying God's Word (Luke 4:16-21; Acts 9:20; 13:5; 15:21; 13:44; 1 Cor. 4:17; Col. 4:15, 16). Not just Sabbath services, but prayer meetings, camp meetings, and other gatherings of God's people provide this opportunity. The life of the church is sustained by the Word of God taught, believed, practiced, and promulgated (Acts 20:28, 32; 1 Thess. 2:13). Jesus addressed His revelation epistles to the seven *churches*, not just to believers at random (Rev. 2 and 3). He ended each letter by saying: "He who has an ear, let him hear what the Spirit says to the churches" (e.g., Rev. 2:11; 3:22, NKJV). He speaks to individual believers, to be sure, but He also has special messages for the corporate benefit of His people. He still speaks to His church today through His ministers who faithfully preach the Word.

Thus the church is the pillar and ground of the truth (1 Tim. 3:15). Those Christians who do not attend church miss that appointed blessing. The church has an obligation to bring some portion of that blessing to those members who cannot attend for various reasons, such as illness or infirmity. A cassette recording of the church service can be a real blessing to such.

Church is a place for the reverent and quiet contemplation of God (Ps. 27:4). It is not always necessary for some music or activity to fill every moment of a church service, as though worshipers need to be incessantly entertained. Reverent silence is hard to find anywhere today. The church should be able to provide that blessing in some measure to those who seek it, while at the same time not having a funereal atmosphere (Ps. 46:10; Hab. 2:20; Zech. 2:13).

Church is a place to which we bring our tithes and offerings to God as an act of worship and practical devotion to His cause (2 Kings 12:4-11; 2 Chron. 24; 31:5-10; Ps. 96:8; Mal. 3:10; Acts 4:32-37).

Church is a place for singing God's praise and for sharing testimonies of rejoicing and thanksgiving (2 Chron. 5:11-14; Ps. 22:22; 100:4; 122:1-4; 149:1, 2). Such worship echoes the praises that sound in heaven (Rev. 4:6-11; 5:11, 12; 7:9-12). Therefore, we should ask God to so anoint us that our praises and songs will accord with the worship activities of heaven.

"The church of God below is one with the church of God above. Believers on earth and the beings in heaven who have never fallen constitute one church. . . . The praise and thanksgiving from the worshipers below is taken up in the heavenly anthem, and praise and rejoicing sound through the heavenly courts because Christ has not died in vain for the fallen sons of Adam. . . .

"The temple of God is opened in heaven, and the threshold is flushed with the glory which is for every church that will love God and keep His commandments. We need to study, to meditate, and to pray. Then we shall have spiritual eyesight to discern the inner courts of the celestial temple. We shall catch the themes of song and thanksgiving of the heavenly choir round about the throne. When Zion shall arise and shine, her light will be most penetrating, and precious songs of praise and thanksgiving will be heard in the assemblies of the saints. Murmuring and complaining over little disappointments and difficulties will cease. As we apply the golden eyesalve we shall see the glories beyond. Faith will cut through the heavy shadow of Satan, and we shall see our Advocate offering up the incense of His own merits in our behalf. When we see this as it is, as the Lord desires us to see it, we shall be filled with a sense of the immensity and diversity of the love of God.

"God teaches us that we should assemble in His house to cultivate the attributes of perfect love. This will fit the dwellers of earth for the mansions that Christ has gone to prepare for all who love Him. There they will assemble in the sanctuary from Sabbath to Sabbath, from one new moon to another, to unite in loftiest strains of song, in praise and thanksgiving to Him who sits upon the throne, and to the Lamb for ever and ever" *(Testimonies,* vol. 6, pp. 366-368).

Endeavoring to live in harmony with heaven's fellowship, the church voluntarily adheres to practical standards of conduct and lifestyle defined or clearly implied in Scripture. This is probably the most controversial and variable aspect of the church's life and witness. But it need not be so with regard to principle, because God's Word stands sure, pure, and everlasting. Practices may vary from age to age and culture to culture, but God's principles are universal and unchanging. He desires to raise up a peculiar people, zealous of good works and zealous to let His good work of vital transformation progress without obstruction in their lives. We embrace Christian standards to give God free rein to live out His life within us, without distortion or distraction resulting from misguided ideas and faulty practices on our part (1 Thess. 4:1-8; 5:22-24).

That is why informed and converted Seventh-day Adventists

joyfully accept God's counsel on such practical matters as diet, dress, adornment, association, recreation, education, and every issue that has a practical bearing on our witness for Christ and our spiritual development into His image (read 1 Cor. 15:33, 34; 2 Cor. 6:14-7:1; Phil. 4:8; 1 Tim. 2:9-11; 1 Peter 3:1-8). It is not just external change in behavior that God seeks, but a glorious transformation of character. He wants us to be richly adorned not with outward splendor, but with the gracious attributes of His own nature.

The church does not invent arbitrary standards. It dare not be any stricter in its rules for living than the Bible is, but likewise it dare not be any more permissive than Scripture. Its duty is to teach and obey the Word, no matter how much contempt humanity in general and apostate Christendom in particular may cast upon divine counsel, stigmatizing it as antiquated or declaring it to be abolished by Christ's death on Calvary. Christ's death on the cross was not to weaken practical godliness or dismiss it as irrelevant, but to establish it forever on an incorruptible, heaven-empowered plane in our hearts. But sanctification is a process of growth, and we need to give each other time and space to develop into the fullness of the stature of God's children, without being coercive or critical.

The Lord wants us to be attractive, convincing stewards of His grace. His program is not one of demand for rigid rectitude, but an offer to envelop us with His life so that we might live in holy partnership with Him, conformed to His character and will. Any other approach to Christianity is dry and forced; it is sterile and unfulfilling. He has saved us and called us with a holy calling, not according to our works, but according to His own purpose and grace (2 Tim. 1:9). And that purpose and grace are replete with endless delight and rich value.

True Christianity frees us to use our God-given talents in pursuits that will bless others. We do not have to suffer from addicting habits that hurt ourselves and our families. We do not have to be enslaved by attitudes that crush our capacity to love and serve humanity. We do not have to live in the death grip of self-centeredness that makes us think first and last of our own feelings, our own desires, and our own needs. As Christians we are stewards of the marvelous mysteries of God's truth and grace. We are also ambassadors for Christ; our lives are elevated to the dignity of a holy mission. When we capture this vision, no standard of God's Word will seem too high. And we will always know that the power of His Spirit is ready to strengthen us to do God's will joyfully from the heart. Our question will not be "Do I have to do this; do I have to make that change?" but "Is it really my privilege to follow God so closely that I can obey Him in all things?"

"God will accept only those who are determined to aim high. He places every human agent under obligation to do his best. Moral perfection is required of all. Never should we lower the standard of righteousness in order to accommodate inherited or cultivated tendencies to wrongdoing. We need to understand that imperfection of character is sin. All righteous attributes of character dwell in God as a perfect, harmonious whole, and everyone who receives Christ as a personal Saviour is privileged to possess these attributes. . . . Be ambitious for the Master's glory, to cultivate every grace of character. . . . To everyone engaged in this work Christ says, I am at your right hand to help you" (*Christ's Object Lessons*, pp. 330-332).

This is no high-pressure program, but the bequest of divine love. God woos; He doesn't whip us into holy living (Hosea 14:4-9). True, He does discipline us, but always and only in love for our eternal benefit so that we may represent Him faithfully and attractively to the world (Rev. 3:18-21). And that is the whole idea of Christian standards. We want our Saviour's grace to shine through our lives with undimmed luster and unblemished beauty. After all, He is preparing His people as a royal bride for His kingdom!

But every Christian knows from personal experience that the life of faith is not a romantic dream. At times in our experience the "consecration, submission, and sacrifices" that must be made "seem like taking the very lifeblood from the heart" (*That I May Know Him*, p. 280).

Some years ago during a construction project in South America many of the workers were stricken with malaria. Not knowing the cause, but recognizing that it was from something in the environment, the chief engineer resolved to destroy the surrounding jungle by fire. So thick was the foliage that it took six months to accomplish the job. The team of workers so thoroughly eradicated life from the soil that not a plant remained. In time the construction project was completed and the workers left.

Two years went by, and the first form of plant life to emerge from that burned-over ground was a flower of such rare beauty as to command the admiration of all who saw it. The flower was carefully dug from the ground and submitted to floral experts for classification. But no one had ever seen another flower like it; it stood alone in its unique beauty and grace.

And so it is with our lives. We are baptized with the Holy Spirit and fiery trials so that we may bring forth distinctive fruit for the glory of God and be free from the malaria of pride even in our religious lives, where uncrucified selfhood is often hidden behind the luxuriant foliage of assumed piety (Zech. 13:9; Mal. 3:1-5; Luke 3:16).

Like a
Mighty Army

10

One day a group of eager, ambitious ministerial students were discussing their future careers. All envisioned themselves as top-flight evangelists and superb administrators. They knew they were an elite corps with extraordinary abilities. But the all-absorbing question was Who was the most gifted and capable person among them? When they graduated, who would emerge as the rightful leader, the CEO of the up-and-coming denomination whose membership was soon likely to swell into the millions, thanks to their miracle-working powers and anointed preaching? Each person, piously convinced of his own superiority, was angered that the others did not recognize it, and quit haggling about the matter.

What did their Teacher do? Flunk them? Expel them and start a new movement? Give them a final examination and post their comparative scores? He did none of these things. Firmly but kindly He corrected them and demonstrated in the most appealing and consistent way the qualities He wished to see them cultivate through His grace. And He kept pointing them to His cross and its meaning for their own and others' salvation.

In the process of this instruction these students were obliged to surrender some of their most cherished notions. Eventually all but one of them underwent a profound revolution in their thinking and experience, which made it possible for them all to exceed their highest ambitions without having to be in competition with each other.

Imperfect individuals, laboring under absurd misconceptions of their holy calling and misconstruing the basic principles of their

Teacher—could any good thing come out of their joint enterprise? No lasting good, unless they underwent a complete change of attitude and behavior. They experienced that change, more radically than anyone but God could have foreseen. Calvary and the baptism of the Holy Spirit made the difference.

Through the conscientious, Spirit-filled work of these men from Pentecost onward, the world was evangelized in a generation (Acts 17:6; Rom. 10:16-18; Col. 1:23) without the benefit of rapid transit, radio, television, printing presses, telephones, and other more recent inventions that so greatly facilitate evangelism today. Yet the gospel traveled as on wings of fire, because the early church was filled with the Holy Spirit (see the many references to this in the book of Acts, e.g., Acts 2:4; 4:31).

After a scant two generations (A.D. 31-100), however, that celestial fervor dimmed to near extinction. This was not because of any depletion of Heaven's power, any dwindling in the supplies of grace, but because the believers had "left their first love" (Rev. 2:4). This departure was no small crisis, because the very essence of Christianity, the lifeblood of the church, is love. "He who does not love does not know God, for God is love" (1 John 4:8, NKJV).

Did God make a mistake in establishing the church? Was it a brave but quixotic venture with a perfect mission and a perfect message, but doomed to failure because of its imperfect medium—people who fall short of God's glory? In the history of the church we find the best and most important news that could ever be told, sent by messengers who often muffle, misinterpret, mislay, and sometimes mangle that very news. What accounts for this contradictory situation? God did not blunder. He perfectly foresaw the entire history of the church from its beginning to end, as Christ's letters to the seven churches (Rev. 2 and 3) plainly reveal.

God fully comprehends the challenges involved in sending the gospel to the world. The gospel is more than a system of correct ideas, and a flawless methodology of service; it is the vitalizing power of God taking hold of human hearts and transforming them into the image of God, which has been nearly obliterated by sin (Rom. 1:16, 17). This great change in human lives is hindered by three major obstacles:

1. Satan's opposition to it (Rev. 12:17).

2. The world's opposition to it (John 15:18-21).

3. Every human being's natural resistance to it (Rom. 8:7).

The church is God's divinely appointed refuge for the restoration of spiritually damaged lives. Those who compose its membership are in the process of being reconstructed from almost hopeless ruin. Many patients seem worse while under treatment than they did beforehand, but this does not invalidate the treatments or condemn the attending physicians.

It is the nature of the church militant that the full array of human imperfection is displayed in its midst. Only those church members who really want the gospel to take full effect in their lives are entirely restored. They do not settle for what is customary on earth, or in church, but for what is approved in heaven. In every age they have constituted the true church, the remnant that shall be part of God's eternal kingdom (Isa. 1:8, 9; Micah 7:18; Zeph. 3:13).

The church militant would be the church defeated and desolated if God were not in her midst. We could not be Christians without Jesus in our lives, and the church could not be His body without Christ at its head diffusing His life throughout the body (Eph. 1:22, 23; Col. 1:18). Those who reject His life transfused into their own are branches that God shall break off (John 15:1-6). For without the sap of divine grace flowing through the hearts of church members, they are lifeless wood, like broomsticks, only less serviceable. Yet none should judge the case of others prematurely. God can make dead trees live again, and bring dead bones to life (Job 14:7-9; Eze. 37:3-10). After all, Christ, who is the Resurrection and the Life, doesn't reserve all His resurrection power until the Second Coming (see Eph. 1:19-23; 2:1-6). He is the sustaining life of His church. Therefore it behooves the members of the church militant to refrain from judging fellow members, and to help one another along the pathway to heaven (Gal. 6:1, 2).

The problems of the church militant do not stem from any defectiveness in God's design for it, but from the profoundly disordering effects of sin upon humanity and Satan's relentless efforts to make matters steadily worse. Without the church, humanity would remain in a state of hopeless depravity. Despite all the present weaknesses in the church, God channels through it His regenerative power to the world. Christ does more good for and through His church than Satan does harm. Meanwhile we are to account Christ's long-suffering not to be permissiveness, incompetence, or disengagement, but gracious opportunity for salvation (see 2 Peter 3:15). He bears long with us all, because the best of us have more weaknesses and failings than we can number (Ps. 40:11, 12; Rom. 3:9-19), and He will not restore our souls any faster than He has our consent and desire. Church members or not, we have no idea how sinful we really are until we fully awaken to Christ's righteousness (1 Cor. 15:34).

Therefore it is the height of folly to be angry with the church for its imperfections. If we are, it is virtually unmistakable evidence that we are blind to our own sins and failings. Many who take it upon themselves to criticize and reprove the church are living in a state of entrenched disobedience to God's will. Christ reproved people, and so did the prophets, but they did so under divine inspiration. Not all rebukes administered in the name of the Lord are divinely inspired. Often they are the fruit of an irritable temper that is as quick to berate someone for a minor slip as for a major offense. Hatefulness and a faultfinding spirit do not become miraculously ennobled by being cloaked in robes of religious fervor.

The wheat and tares are both to grow together until the harvest (Matt. 13:30). It is tares that are bitter, not the golden grain under God's cultivation. It is not those who are feeding on the unleavened bread of sincerity and truth who are reproachful and condemnatory, but rather those who indulge in the leaven of malice and wickedness. They are spurred on by the accuser of the brethren (1 Cor. 5:8; 2 Cor. 2:1-11; Rev. 12:10). We need to examine our own selves to see whether *we* are in the faith, and we must abandon the futile work of trying to pull out the mote we see in everyone else's eye when a beam is in our own.

"If ever there was a time when those who have a knowledge of present truth should find their bearings, it is the present time. Although no one is to move independently of his brethren, yet each one must gain a knowledge of his own condition, his exact bearings. The question that each one should ask himself is 'What is my relation to God?'

"It is conformity to the world that is causing our people to lose their bearings. The perversion of right principles has not been brought about suddenly. The angel of the Lord presented this matter to me in symbols. It seemed as if a thief were stealthily moving in closer and still closer, and gradually but surely stealing away the identity of God's work by leading our brethren to conform to worldly policies. . . .

"The Lord expects us to make most diligent efforts to free ourselves of the worldly spirit that has come in among us. . . . The Lord calls for a reformation. . . .

"Remember that in preparing yourselves for the heavenly kingdom, you are preparing others" *(The Upward Look,* p. 202).

This passage is worth analyzing closely. A careful consideration of it will help us come to terms with the problems that exist among us as a people—worldliness, lack of correct spiritual bearings, Laodicean cloudiness of vision. But a correct understanding of this passage will steer us away from the fatally wrong course of lashing out at the church and rising up to denounce her leaders. This is not the heroic thing to do. The real heroism is to apply the counsel to ourselves—to each individually discover our *own* bearings in relation to Christ, to each make our *own* calling and election sure, to each engage in a solid work of reform in our *own* lives. (Carefully read 1 Timothy 4:16; see also Matthew 7:1-4; 2 Corinthians 13:5; and *Thoughts From the Mount of Blessing,* pp. 123-129.)

It is a thousand times easier for the carnal heart to denounce sin in others than to renounce sin itself. This is especially true if our sins are of the Pharisaic order—no immorality, no alcoholism, no dancing, no card playing, no forbidden foods, but also no love, no mercy, no abasement of self-pride before Calvary's cross. To be an "orthodox" Adventist without having the love of Jesus is to be a moral iceberg. Even so, those who are *not* locked in the grip of arrogant orthodoxy have no license to despise those who are. God's cause shall never need our wormwood and gall to prosper, and contempt is no substitute for redemptive action. The gospel authorizes and liberates us to love as Christ loves. One truly converted person among us who consistently exhibits the grace and goodness of the Saviour will have a revolutionary effect in the church. Through that person's influence pharisees, publicans, liberals, conservatives, vacillators, and sinners of every grade and shade will be converted to Christ.

Micah's counsel to ancient Israel has lost none of its validity or effectiveness: "He has shown you, O man, what is good; and what does the Lord require of you but to do justly, to love mercy, and to walk humbly with your God?" (Micah 6:8, NKJV). Those who sincerely love God and His truth pray to see purity and consecration manifest in every facet of the church's life, and they pray to see these qualities manifest in their own lives. They sigh and cry for it, but they do not let their mourning degenerate into accusatory bitterness and vituperative alienation (Eze. 9). Any bitterness they have is one of contrition for wounding Christ's heart by their own failure to represent Him properly to others (Zech. 12:10-14).

"All our zeal will not be successful in making the church militant as pure as the church triumphant. The Lord forbids us to proceed in any violent way against those whom we think erring, and we are not to deal out excommunications and denunciations to those who are faulty.

"Finite man is likely to misjudge character, but God does not leave the work of judgment and pronouncing upon character to those who are not fitted for it. We are not to say what constitutes the wheat, and what the tares. The time of the harvest will fully determine the character of the two classes specified under the figure of the tares and the wheat. The work of separation is given to the angels of God, and not committed into the hands of any man" *(Testimonies to Ministers,* p. 47).

Despite its undeniable weaknesses and deficiencies, God's church has throughout its history been the light of the world (Matt. 5:14; Eph. 5:8; Rev. 1:20). Through the labor of the church, the gospel has continued to be preached, even when its witnesses were clothed in the sackcloth of social dishonor and religious persecution and the light they bore was partially obscured by the mists of satanically imposed darkness during the long ages of apostasy (Rev. 2:18-28; 11:3).

Drawing on Bible imagery (Amos 9:11; Acts 15:14-17; Eph. 2:20-22), Ellen White referred to the building of God's church as the erection of His temple. Consider her encouraging view of the church militant:

"Kings and governors, priests and rulers, sought to destroy the temple of God. But in the face of imprisonment, torture, and death, faithful men carried the work forward; and the structure grew, beautiful and symmetrical. At times the workmen were almost blinded by the mists of superstition that settled around them. At times they were almost overpowered by the violence of their opponents. But with unfaltering faith and unfailing courage they pressed on with the work.

"One after another the foremost of the builders fell by the hand of the enemy. Stephen was stoned; James was slain by the sword; Paul was beheaded; Peter was crucified; John was exiled. Yet the church grew. New workers took the place of those who fell, and stone after stone was added to the building. Thus slowly ascended the temple of the church of God.

"Centuries of fierce persecution followed the establishment of the Christian church, but there were never wanting men who counted the work of building God's temple dearer than life itself. . . .

"The enemy of righteousness left nothing undone in his effort to stop the work committed to the Lord's builders. But God 'left not himself without witness.' Acts 14:17. Workers were raised up who ably defended the faith once delivered to the saints. History bears record to the fortitude and heroism of these [men and women]. Like the apostles, many of them fell at their post, but the building of the temple went steadily forward. The workmen were slain, but the work advanced. The Waldenses, John Wycliffe, Huss and Jerome, Martin Luther and Zwingli, Cranmer, Latimer, and Knox, the Huguenots, John and Charles Wesley, and a host of others brought to the foundation material that will endure throughout eternity. And in later years those who have so nobly endeavored to promote the circulation of God's word, and those who by their service in heathen lands have prepared the way for the proclamation of the last great message—these also have helped to rear the structure.

"Through the ages that have passed since the days of the apostles, the building of God's temple has never ceased. We may look back through the centuries and see the living stones of which it is composed gleaming like jets of light through the darkness of error and superstition. Throughout eternity these precious jewels will shine with increasing luster, testifying to the power of the truth of God" *(The Acts of the Apostles,* pp. 597, 598).

As we can see, the church militant is not so called because it is belligerent, but because it is besieged. It is called militant not because it is angry, but because it is agonized by outward assaults and internal weaknesses. Militant because it refuses to be discouraged by the most hopeless-seeming prospects. Militant because, in the face of all opposition, it keeps its eye steadily on Christ, the Captain of its salvation. Militant because it fights the good fight of faith and triumphs over all the enemy's devices and depredations. Militant because the kingdom of heaven suffers violence, and the violent take it by force (Matt. 11:12). This is the violence of a holy resolve to let the grace of Christ triumph over all evil without and within. Those who are true members of the church militant fight only with the spiritual weaponry of God's Word and prayer (Eph. 6:18; 2 Cor. 10:3-5). They don't turn their weapons against the church or society, but against all forms of evil that war against the salvation of souls and the grace, peace, and dignity of life.

The spiritual militancy of the church must not be contaminated with caustic attitudes or rude behavior—that would disgrace its mission by misrepresenting the Lord of glory. "The life of Christ was a life charged with a divine message of the love of God, and He longed intensely to impart this love to others in rich measure. Compassion beamed from His countenance, and His conduct was characterized by grace, humility, truth, and love. *Every member of His church militant must manifest the same qualities, if he would join the church triumphant.* The love of Christ is so broad, so full of glory, that in comparison to it, everything that men esteem as great dwindles into insignificance. When we obtain a view of it, we exclaim, O the depth of the riches of the love that God bestowed upon men in the gift of His only-begotten Son!" *(Fundamentals of Christian Education,* p. 179; italics supplied).

This is the only heaven-approved militancy—the exercise of pure love that drives out the darkness of sin and error and amid the bleakness of this sin-blighted world makes "straight in the desert a highway for our God" (Isa. 40:3; see also verses 4-11).

Many years ago a famous Adventist minister, Dudley Canright, developed doubts about the message he had for so many years ably advocated. Egotism and dissatisfaction with the unpopular aspects of our message made him restless. He craved a wider audience, a larger fame than he could obtain by continuing as an Adventist.

Thus he found it easy to see more and more faults in the church, more and more reasons he should leave it. The Lord presented his case to Ellen White in vision. Here is a part of what she saw and wrote to Canright:

"I had an impressive dream last night. I thought that you were on a strong vessel, sailing on very rough waters. Sometimes the waves beat over the top, and you were drenched with water. You said, 'I shall get off; this vessel is going down.' 'No,' said one who appeared to be the captain, 'this vessel sails into the harbor. She will never go down.' But you answered: 'I shall be washed overboard. As I am neither captain or mate, who cares? I shall take my chances on that vessel you see yonder.' Said the captain: 'I shall not let you go there, for I know that vessel shall strike the rocks before she reaches the harbor.' You straightened yourself up, and said with great positiveness: 'This vessel will become a wreck; I can see it just as plain as can be.' The captain looked upon you with piercing eye, and said firmly: 'I shall not permit you to lose your life by taking that boat. The timbers of her framework are worm-eaten, and she is a deceptive craft. If you had more knowledge you could discern between the spurious and the genuine, the holy and that appointed to utter ruin'" *(Testimonies,* vol. 5, pp. 571, 572).

Canright ultimately did not heed the admonition. Repudiating the Sabbath and all the other salient features of our message, he made shipwreck of his faith. He left the church and died a broken, lonely, obscure man. But the church against which he turned has continued its message and mission with unabated strength, taking the light of present truth to the whole world.

About 15 years later the Lord gave Ellen White another vision regarding the church's duty to meet a serious theological crisis that rocked the entire denomination. She called it the alpha of apostasy. Its two chief characteristics were pantheism (the idea that we are innately divine) and muted antinomianism (key into your true inward holiness and you need no commandments, no codified principles, to define moral conduct). This apostasy included more than flawed doctrinal beliefs. It was riddled with flawed attitudes, once more heavily entwined with egotism and a flaming thirst for personal fame (see Num. 16:1-10; 2 Cor. 11:13-15). Some leaders were involved in this heresy. Other leaders, including Ellen White, opposed it. (For a more detailed consideration of this subject, read *Selected Messages,* book 1, pp. 193-208.) It was not wholesale denominational apostasy, but it was a conflict that threatened to divide the church. How should the matter be dealt with? Expediency, compromise, suspended discussion?

The Lord guided the church to a proper response through a dramatic vision He gave to Ellen White.

"Shortly before I sent out the testimonies regarding the efforts of the enemy to undermine the foundations of our faith through the dissemination of seductive theories, I had read an incident about a ship in a fog meeting an iceberg. For several nights I slept but little. I seemed to be bowed down as a cart beneath sheaves. One night a scene was clearly presented before me. A vessel was upon the waters, in a heavy fog. Suddenly the lookout cried, 'Iceberg just ahead!' There, towering high above the ship, was a gigantic iceberg. An authoritative voice cried out, 'Meet it!' There was not a moment's hesitation. It was a time for instant action. The engineer put on full steam, and the man at the wheel steered the ship straight into the iceberg. With a crash she struck the ice. There was a fearful shock, and the iceberg broke into many pieces, falling with a noise like thunder to the deck. The passengers were violently shaken by the force of the collision, but no lives were lost. The vessel was injured, but not beyond repair. She rebounded from the contact, trembling from stem to stern, like a living creature. Then she moved forward on her way" *(Selected Messages,* book 1, pp. 205, 206).

Ellen White recognized from this dream that it was her duty to meet head-on the fatal, seductive errors that were creeping in among us as a people. The church was severely shaken by this theological crisis of the early 1900s, but it has not only survived—it has also triumphed over every device of the enemy, and shall continue to do so, all voices of doubt notwithstanding. The message we have been entrusted with since the beginning of our movement has lost none of its authority or relevance. In fact, the truth of our message has become increasingly apparent over time. The truth shall triumph, and those who love the truth shall triumph with it!

"We have no discouraging message for the church. Although reproofs and cautions and corrections have been made, yet the church has stood as God's instrumentality to diffuse light. The commandment-keeping people of God have sounded forth a warning to the world. . . . The church of God is a living witness, a continual testimony, to convince men if accepted, to condemn them if resisted and rejected.

"The church must and will shine forth 'fair as the moon, clear as the sun, and terrible as an army with banners' S. of Sol. 6:10" *(Our High Calling,* p. 353).

As the church militant, we have one more major internal crisis to face before we move on to ultimate triumph—the omega of apostasy. It is beyond the scope of this book to discuss that matter in detail. But I will make a few, hopefully constructive, observations here. The omega of apostasy will very likely be a disguised edition of the alpha—the promotion of the idea that as believers we are divinely guided by our sanctified imaginations as something equivalent to the gift of prophecy and that we do not need so much explicit instruction (as from the Bible and Spirit of Prophecy, i.e., legalistic religion) to maintain a consecrated walk with God. We can rejoice in our freedom in Christ without all the constraints of carefully formulated doctrinal beliefs. For some this dish of lies is very inviting, but it is devoid of soul nourishment. It is theological junk food.

This is Satan's final in-house edition of temptingly packaged apostasy for the remnant church. (He offers a more aggressive form of it through Babylon.) We must not be enchanted by the devil's flattering serenades. We are *not* gods, and it is not in us who walk to direct our own steps. So we do well to recognize our privileged yet eternally subordinate status as God's children and to be so filled with the Spirit that God's law becomes a delight to us (Ps. 40:8) instead of being misperceived as a dreary burden.

The amplified instruction in the Spirit of Prophecy is like a road map. When I am traveling over unfamiliar territory I like a map that is full of informative details. I haven't been to heaven before, but that's my goal. If God sees fit to offer me a wealth of information on what to do and what not to do, where to go and where not to go, en route, I want to be attentive, grateful, and obedient to His directions. After all, who knows the helps and hindrances along the way better than He? And while God is communicative, He is not verbose. He wouldn't tell us any more than we need to know to make our heavenward journey a complete success, free from all devilish diversions and snares. What sensible pilgrim wouldn't want to be warned about Satan's deadly traps and informed about those things that brace and refresh the soul?

Obedience to God's Word is not legalism. After all, without Him we can't do anything, and He bestows on us all the grace we need to live by every word that proceeds from His mouth. Can't Christ, the living Word, inscribe His written word on any heart that is supple, yielded, and loyal to Him, loving Him because He first loved us? Isn't that what the new covenant experience offers (Heb. 8:10-12)? Plainly, it is.

"We are God's commandment-keeping people. For the past fifty years [written in 1904] every phase of heresy has been brought to bear upon us, to becloud our minds regarding the teaching of the Word—especially concerning the ministration of Christ in the heavenly sanctuary, and the message of Heaven for these last days, as given by the angels of the fourteenth chapter of Revelation. Messages of every order and kind have been urged upon Seventh-day Adventists, to take the place of the truth which, point by point, has been sought out by prayerful study, and testified to by the miracle-working power of the Lord. But the waymarks which have made us what we are, are to be preserved, and they will be preserved, as God has signified through His Word and the testimony of His Spirit. He calls upon us to hold firmly, with the grip of faith, to the fundamental principles that are based upon unquestionable authority" *(Selected Messages,* book 1, p. 208).

Those who love the Lord and cleave to His changeless counsel will stand as an immovable bulwark against the rough winds of heresy and trial that assail us as a people and are to intensify to the close of time. The church militant learns how to endure hardness as good soldiers of Jesus Christ. Yet the hearts of God's people are not hard; they remain pliable in His hands, but adamant against temptation. Largely misunderstood and misrepresented, His witnesses lovingly continue to let their light shine on all around them. We should never let our goodwill run dry, nor allow any root of bitterness to spring up in us.

John Wesley exemplified this principle well. Many Christians unjustly regarded Methodism for its first 50 years or so as a despicable sect. John Brown, a famous and devoted Christian minister of

Haddington, shared this common misconception of Wesley and his work. On his deathbed he thanked God that he had been spared from becoming entangled with "that man of sin, John Wesley."

Knowing John Brown's opinion of him, Wesley said with forgiving kindness in a sermon, "I hope to meet John Brown in heaven and join him in the praises of God and the Lamb."

We too must not let ourselves feel slighted by those who misunderstand us. Our great effort should be to avoid giving anyone legitimate occasion to think ill of our Christianity (see Acts 24:16). "It must needs be that offences come," Christ said. But on whom did He pronounce a woe? Not on the victim of the offense, but on the perpetrator (Matt. 18:7).

The Lord is desiring to bring us into a harbor of gracious experience. The good ship Zion, His church, is in for a very tempestuous voyage during the last phase of its journey. Organized, worldwide persecution awaits us (Rev. 12:17; 13:11-18). But with Jesus, the Captain of our salvation, at the helm, we shall be guided safely, victoriously into port.

Fear not, weary voyager. Soon you shall be home. Your final passage will not be through earth's troubled waters, but through the wide expanse of serene heavens to the gates of New Jerusalem. And your traveling companions will be your angel, your fellow pilgrims of earth, and the Saviour who guides you over the storm-tossed sea of your life as you brave your way Zionward with God's remnant church.

> Long upon the mountains weary,
> Have the scattered flock been torn;
> Dark the desert paths, and dreary;
> Grievous trials have they borne.
> Now the gathering call is sounding,
> Solemn in its warning voice;
> Union, faith, and love, abounding,
> Bid the little flock rejoice.
>
> Now the light of truth they're seeking,
> In its onward track pursue;
> All the ten commandments keeping,

They are holy, just, and true.
On the words of life they're feeding,
Precious to their taste so sweet;
All their Master's precepts heeding,
Bowing humbly at His feet.

In that light of light and beauty,
In that golden city fair,
Soon its pearly gates they'll enter,
And of all its glories share.
There, divine the soul's expansions;
Free from sin, and death, and pain;
Tears will never dim those mansions
Where the saints immortal reign.

Soon He comes! with clouds descending;
All His saints, entombed arise;
The redeemed, in anthems blending,
Shout their vict'ry thro' the skies.
O, we long for Thine appearing;
Come, O Savior, quickly come!
Blessed hope! our spirits cheering,
Take Thy ransomed children home."

—Annie Smith

The Remnant
of His Heritage

11

The new general was amazed. His Commander-in-chief had ordered him to expel their oppressors from the land. Dutifully the general assembled all the troops he could muster, an emergency militia of 32,000; not an especially formidable host to engage an enemy force of 135,000 battle-hardened warriors. But his Chief told the general to send home all who were afraid to fight. In a few hours the general's army was reduced to 10,000 fighting men—one soldier to 13 of the enemy's. An intimidating ratio, but perhaps not altogether hopeless. Then the Commander-in-chief issued a fresh order. He said His general had too many soldiers. So by an amazing test the general's army was reduced in a few hours to 300, leaving a ratio of one man to 450 of the foe.

Now the human impossibility of obtaining victory was established beyond doubt. Thus the Commander-in-chief was free to lead His general, Gideon, on to victory without question as to its source. Gideon and the children of Israel needed to learn the valuable lesson that there is no restraint to the Lord to save by many or by few (1 Sam. 14:6). The cause that God advocates is ultimately invincible, because truth and love shall triumph over deception and hate (2 Cor. 2:14; 13:8).

Another lesson emerges from the formation of Gideon's army. The 300 who led Israel to victory over the Philistines were chosen because of their single-minded devotion to God's cause. "The men of His choice were the few who would not permit their own wants to delay them in the discharge of duty. The three hundred chosen men not only possessed courage and self-control, but they were men of faith. They had not defiled themselves with idolatry. God could direct them, and through them He could work deliverance for Israel. . . . [God] is honored not so much by great numbers as by the character of those who serve Him" *(Patriarchs and Prophets,* pp. 549, 550).

Only a remnant, a small minority, of Gideon's army was called to lead the way to victory. This was not because of favoritism on God's part, but a result of the fitness of those finally chosen. On at least two separate occasions Jesus said: "Many are called, but few chosen" (Matt. 20:16; 22:14, NKJV). He made this statement on at least two separate occasions (see also Matt. 22:14). His solemn and striking words bear close analysis. First, we should recognize that Jesus was not hinting at some program of arbitrary exclusiveness. He clearly stated that it was not God's will for anyone to be lost (Matt. 18:14). Peter, who came to understand well the breadth and depth of divine mercy, said that God is "not willing that any should perish, but that all should come to repentance" (2 Peter 3:9).

What is meant, then, by the phrase "many are called"? Does this mean that some are not called at all? The comparison of two other texts will help us understand this enigma. Jesus said: "The Son of man came . . . to give his life a ransom for *many*" (Matt. 20:28). Paul said: "Christ Jesus . . . gave himself a ransom for *all*, to be testified in due time" (1 Tim. 2:5, 6). Are these two statements contradictory? Not at all. The *many* for whom He died are sinners, and that is *all* human beings. In a broader sense, the many for whom He died are the universe of morally intelligent beings, including those who never fell. His atoning sacrifice for sinful humanity renders the unfallen immune to all temptation ever to rebel against His will (1 Cor. 4:9; Col. 1:20). The loyal universe has witnessed the fearful degradation and desolation brought on by sin, which originated with the most gifted and enlightened of created beings, Lucifer (Isa. 14:9-20; Eze. 28:1-19).

After the great controversy between good and evil is resolved, no one will ever again be attracted to departing from the way and will of God. All the redeemed and all the sinless worlds that have witnessed the history of redemption will love and trust God on an unshakably secure foundation (Nahum 1:9; Rev. 21:4; 22:3).

In what sense, then, are few *chosen*? Only in the sense that proportionately *few ransomed sinners choose to accept* the benefit. Those who, like Mary, choose the good part (Christ's fellowship and salvation) shall not have it taken away from them (Luke 10:39, 42). But most people are so blinded by sin that they do not recognize the value of the call to salvation, especially when they sense that to accept life in Christ entails death to selfishness and sin (see Luke 14:15-27).

Without doing violence to the intent of Scripture, we could restate Christ's words in Matthew 20:16 and 22:14: "Every sinner is called, but few choose to respond." Those who do respond on God's own terms have always constituted His remnant of followers. These are the "called, chosen, and faithful," who make their "calling and election sure" in Christ by electing to receive, believe, and serve Him and be served by Him according to His knowledge of their need. They do not bargain with God, but unreservedly give themselves to Him, thankful for every change He wants to make in their lives and every blessing He wants to bestow. Christ commissions those who accept Him fully to take His message of salvation to the world, a message divested of the dross of human opinion and the crust of worthless traditions that make void God's law and testimony.

"In a special sense Seventh-day Adventists have been set in the world as watchmen and light bearers. To them has been entrusted the last warning for a perishing world. On them is shining a wonderful light from the word of God. They have been given a work of the most solemn import—the proclamation of the first, second, and third angels' messages. There is no other work of so great importance. They are to allow nothing else to absorb their attention" *(Testimonies,* vol. 9, p. 19).

The message we have to bear is not held in universal favor any more than were the messages of Noah, Elijah, or John the Baptist. Some aspects of truth are welcome to nearly all. Those parts that tell about God's kindness, love, and mercy are easy to accept. But those parts of truth that call for commitment, obedience, and accountability to God and for repentance of sin are generally not so well greeted. And yet Jesus, in reiterating the gospel commission to His disciples, said shortly before His final ascension: "Thus it is written, and thus it was necessary for the Christ to suffer and to rise from the dead the third day, and *that repentance and remission of sin should be preached in His name to all nations*, beginning at Jerusalem. And you are witnesses of these things" (Luke 24:46-48, NKJV). Jesus began His mission with a call to repentance and its corresponding offer of God's forgiveness, and He enlisted disciples to help Him fully publicize this call (see Mark 1:15-18).

As sinners we all need to repent. Repentance so softens the heart that we confess our sins and thus have the way opened to be forgiven and restored (1 John 1:9). Repentance makes the heart supple so that God can impress upon it His own character (Eze. 36:25-31). God's love and goodness lead us to repentance; it is His gift to draw our sin-stricken souls back to Him (Acts 5:31; Rom. 2:4). It makes us workable clay, as it were, to be shaped by God's hands and baked in the furnace of affliction so that we might become suitable vessels through which He can pour out His grace to the world (Isa. 48:10; 64:8; 2 Tim. 2:21).

We become partakers of the divine nature by yielding to this work of divine grace (Isa. 64:5, 6; Heb. 12:10; 2 Peter 1:4). But to receive this honor we must humbly receive His Spirit's work (Prov. 3:34; Matt. 5:5; 11:28-30; 1 Peter 5:5). The proud heart is too selfish and arrogant to admit its need for salvation; too haughty to learn from a humble Saviour; too self-justifying to acknowledge the need to repent and be justified by God's forgiving grace; too absorbed in sin to want to give up its self-gratifying propensities and practices.

That is why Noah's message met with ridicule and contempt. That is why Elijah's call to draw near to God in repentant obedience was not readily welcomed. That is why only the repentant truly accepted John the Baptist's message by the Jordan and Peter's message at Pentecost (Mark 1:4, 5; Acts 2:36-42). These champions of truth gave no flattering call, but an earnest appeal to turn to God in contrition and to rely solely on Christ for salvation. They exalted the Messiah as the Lamb of God who takes away the sin of the world (John 1:29; Acts 3:12-21).

And God's last-day messengers, endowed with the spirit and power of Elijah, as was John the Baptist (Mal. 4:4, 5), also faithfully proclaim to the world Christ's call to repentance and belief in the gospel, thereby bringing the commission of worldwide evangelism to its glorious completion.

The present truth proclamation that the hour of His judgment is come awakens morally rational people to abandon every un-Christlike way and receive the offered gift of Christ's righteousness. This response will be more frequently seen when we preach the message of God's judgment in the context of His self-sacrificing love and the power of His grace to save us from all sin and enable us to do His will (Titus 2:14).

"When we have a realization of our weakness, we learn to depend upon a power not inherent. Nothing can take so strong a hold on the heart as the abiding sense of our responsibility to God. Nothing reaches so fully down to the deepest motives of conduct as a sense of the pardoning love of Christ" *(The Desire of Ages,* p. 493).

God's remnant church is commissioned to carry the complete, unadulterated gospel to the world. What are the special characteristics that distinguish the remnant from nominal Christendom and make their message convincing? The Bible clearly addresses this question. About a half dozen terms are translated by the term *remnant* in the King James Version of the Bible. For all these different words the meaning is essentially the same: "what is left over," "what remains," "remainder," "remnant." (See "Remnant" in the *Seventh-day Adventist Bible Dictionary.* It points out that in reference to God's professed people, the remnant have been those who either remain loyal to God in times of apostasy and defection or repentantly return to their former loyalty [e.g., 2 Chron. 30:6; Isa. 1:9; 10:20; Eze. 6:8, 9].) They are also those who survive calamity, pestilence, destruction through God's intervention, and grace (2 Kings 19:30, 31; Ezra 9:13, 14; Isa. 46:3, 4). Never in the majority, the remnant are those who hold on to God with resolute desire to honor and obey Him, whatever adversities may befall (Rom. 9:27-30; 11:1-5; Rev. 7:1-4; 14:1-5). To this remnant collectively, the faithful of every generation, the Messiah will come as Redeemer and King (Isa. 10:20-23; 11:10-12:6; Heb. 11:33-40).

Revelation 12:17 states that the remnant keep the commandments of God and have the testimony of Jesus. Obviously they keep the commandments only through God's grace, for there is no other way (Rom. 6:14-22). The faith of Jesus is the power by which they appropriate this grace (Rom. 3:31; 8:4; Rev. 14:12). They find God's grace sufficient not simply to cover up their deficiencies, but to confer upon them the power of the new covenant: God's law in their hearts and minds, direct access to Him through Christ, and for-giveness of sin (Heb. 8:10-12). The premier quality of the remnant is that they have keyed into the true power and purpose of grace (Micah 7:18-20; Eph. 2:8-10; Titus 2:11-14). This is why Paul refers to the continuance of a "*remnant according to the election of grace*" (Rom. 11:5).

Converted Laodiceans (representing the last phase of church history) recapture in full this often-forgotten and obscured truth. By complete acceptance of the counsel of the True Witness to Laodicea, they repent and receive the gold of faith, by which they appropriate the white robe of Christ's righteousness, and receive the Holy Spirit, through which they intimately apply God's Word to their own lives (Rev. 3:18-21; cf. 1 Peter 1:7; Rev. 19:7, 8; 1 John 2:27; John 14:26).

Because they welcome the Spirit's counsel and transforming power, the remnant are completely honest in their relationship with God and everyone else. "The remnant of Israel shall do no unrigh-teousness and speak no lies, nor shall a deceitful tongue be found in their mouth; for they shall feed their flocks and lie down, and no one shall make them afraid" (Zeph. 3:13, NKJV). This passage clearly parallels Revelation's character description of the 144,000 (Rev. 14:1-5), a people in whose mouths no guile is found. They stand without fault before God's throne. Christ is within the hearts of the 144,000; thus they follow Him wherever He goes and live by every word that proceeds from His mouth. This is the essential quality of the remnant (see John 6:60-69). Out of Christ-filled hearts they bear vibrant witness to His glory, proclaiming the three angels' messages of Revelation 14.

While God's remnant have always been the special object of Satan's malice and assaults, this is especially true for the last-day remnant, in whom the full power of God's salvation is displayed. Satan tries to thwart God's work in their lives by launching a furi-ous warfare against them (see Rev. 12:17). But his rage and malice serve only to consolidate the remnant in their loyalty to Jesus and love for one another. So powerful will be the remnant's connection with God and their witness for Him that He will work through them, against all opposition, to call His people out of Babylon (Rev. 14:1-12; 18:1-4). All who in loyal response to God's call leave Babylon's fellowship and refuse the mark of the beast will bravely join the persecuted remnant (Joel 2:32). Their love for God and His Word will override their fears and strengthen them for the day of ultimate deliverance, when Jesus comes (1 John 2:5, 6; 4:17, 18; Rev. 14:13, 14; 15:1-4; 19:1-13; cf. Jer. 23:1-3; 31:6-13; Zeph. 3:12-20).

The remnant have a special responsibility to press together in bearing the light of the three angels' messages to the world, a task that calls for consecrated unity of belief and action. This need for united effort in the pursuit of one aim is demonstrated by a historic rescue operation. One stormy night off England's coast a ship carrying many passengers became wedged between two rocks that jutted from the heaving waters. All night long the frightened passengers prayed and hoped that someone might come to their rescue.

When morning broke, the inhabitants of a nearby fishing village on the coast saw the ship in its dangerous plight. Using a special harpoon cannon, they shot weighted ropes over to the ship. The crew quickly fastened the ropes to the prow, which was facing toward the shore. The men in the village then pulled the ropes with all their strength, but the ship would not move.

When all the women of the village joined the men in pulling on the ropes, the ship moved forward slightly, but all additional exertions were unavailing. Exhausted, they all sat down on the shore, but tried again and again between rests. Still the ship would not move another inch. At last someone had the idea of asking all the children of the village to help pull the ropes. When the children joined the adults in pulling, they all had enough strength *together* to loosen the ship and draw it safely ashore.

Our work as a church calls for the committed participation of every member. Our task is to pull people on to the shore of a saving relationship with Jesus Christ. We cannot do this work in our own strength, but only in the power of the One who strengthens us with all might by His Spirit (Eph. 3:16; cf. Col. 1:28, 29). When we unite with God in laboring for souls, His Spirit works in us mightily to touch and transform human hearts. And when we unite with one another to this same end, our individual effectiveness is exponentially increased (Eccl. 4:9-12; Isa. 52:1, 2, 7-10).

To make our work easier and more effective, the Lord has entrusted to His last-day remnant the guiding light of the gift of prophecy (Rev. 12:17; 19:10; 22:9), a gift that we recognize was specially manifest in the writings of Ellen G. White. Ellen White is not our goddess or idol, but an instrument God used to give valuable counsel to His church to help us carry out our evangelistic mission to the world in these last difficult and challenging days. It is beyond the scope of this book to give a detailed study on this gift to the church, but for a highly readable and informative introduction to the work and writings of Ellen White, I recommend to the reader a booklet entitled *A Gift of Light*, by Roger Coon, available at Adventist Book Centers everywhere. Suffice it to say here that millions of Adventists accept the writings of Ellen White as inspired by the Holy Spirit, because they thoroughly harmonize with Scripture, and their influence is to draw readers to Christ and His Word (consider 2 Chron. 20:20; 1 Cor. 14:32; 1 Thess. 5:19-21).

Notice these interesting representative statements from Ellen White about the Bible: "We should not take the testimony of any man as to what the Scriptures teach, but should study the words of God for ourselves. . . . The mind will enlarge if it is employed in tracing out the relation of the subject of the Bible, comparing scripture with scripture and spiritual things with spiritual. . . .

"There is nothing more calculated to strengthen the intellect than the study of the Scriptures. No other book is so potent to elevate the thoughts, to give vigor to the faculties, as the broad, ennobling truths of the Bible. If God's word were studied as it should be, men would have a breadth of mind, a nobility of character, and a stability of purpose rarely seen in these times" *(Steps to Christ,* pp. 89, 90).

"The people of God are directed to the Scriptures as their safeguard against the influence of false teachers and the delusive power of spirits of darkness. . . . None but those who have fortified the mind with the truths of the Bible will stand through the last great conflict" *(The Great Controversy,* pp. 593, 594).

The remnant are precisely those people to whom the Word of the Lord is authoritative and precious, the guiding light of their lives, which are bound up with the interests of God's kingdom (Haggai 1:12, 13; John 6:60-67). Their whole aim in life is to follow Christ and encourage others to join them on their heavenward journey.

Have you chosen to follow the Lamb on this upward path? It is the highway cast up for the ransomed of the Lord, and it is paved with love for all who continue on it. Follow this way to its end, and you shall have an abundant entrance into the everlasting kingdom of our Lord and Saviour Jesus Christ.

Yet Shall Not
the Least Grain Fall

12

One midsummer's night in 1971 two men were sleeping in the bedroom of a ground floor apartment. One slept on a cot; the other on the floor. Because it was an unusually warm evening for San Francisco, they had the window wide open. About 2:00 in the morning a startling commotion awakened the men. Five plainclothes police officers, guns drawn, were entering the room one by one through the open window. They had a warrant to search the whole apartment for drugs.

Before turning in for the night, one of the men had laid a plastic bag of marijuana in plain view on top of the television. Next to the marijuana he put a bag of currants that his mother, who lived across town, had given him earlier that evening.

One of the officers, sighting the bags, swooped down on the nearest one and triumphantly exclaimed, "Aha! I've found their stash. Looks like hashish. Now they're busted."

A second officer snatched the bag, sniffed its contents, and threw it down with a curse, saying, "It's only raisins!"

Neither of the embarrassed narcotics officers was inclined to examine the second bag, which had the incriminating substance. Instead, like tornadoes they went through the whole house, throwing down everything in sight, gashing cushions, emptying drawers in their frantic search for drugs, cursing and threatening the startled occupants all the while.

When the police left, both men stood astonished. Badly shaken by the raid, they each had a different final reaction. One of the men became more firmly entrenched in his law-defying conduct and continued the lifestyle that made him a subject of police attention. The other soon afterward changed his life, feeling that this night of horror was ample warning to disentangle himself from living outside the law. This shaking, sifting experience sent these two friends on diverging paths. The same occurrence, shared at the same time, produced opposite results that depended on each man's personal response.

The Bible tells us that in the last days of earth's history everything and everyone will be tested by a shaking for the purpose of revealing that which is unshakable—Christ's kingdom, the principles of His truth, and those who abide in His truth, having intimate fellowship with Him (see Heb. 12:26, 27). Those things that can be shaken must be eliminated from the lives of God's people. They must shake loose of every restraint that keeps them from rapidly progressing heavenward and from helping others along the way.

It is to reveal to us the true character of our spiritual experience that the Lord permits and produces the shaking. It is to our advantage to discover our weaknesses and deficiencies while we can remedy them through His grace, rather than after our cases are eternally decided. In this age of superficiality and soothing, soporific religion, the shaking is necessary. After all, Laodiceans are in a drowse that deceptively resembles wakefulness. We need to be stirred from our lethargy. Belief in the truth is not enough. We must be aroused by it to soul-winning action. Nor ought we overlook the deep inworkings of the power of truth in our own lives.

"There is a great amount of truth professed, but truth practiced in relieving our fellow men is of great influence, reaching unto heaven, and compassing eternity. Every soul in our world is on trial; every man's experience, the common life history, tells in unmistakable language whether he is a doer of Christ's words and His works. There is constantly recurring a large array of little things that God alone sees; to act out in these things the principles of truth will bring a precious reward. The great and important things are recognized by nearly all, but the knitting of these things with the supposedly smaller things of life and closely connecting them as one is too rarely done by professed Christians. Religion is too much profession, and too little reality. . . . Truth, precious truth, is Jesus in the life, a living, active principle" *(This Day With God,* p. 224).

It is to establish, strengthen, and settle us in the truth that the shaking comes. And those who reject the power of truth and sovereignty of God will collapse in the shaking, because their religious experience, no matter how impressive it appears, is an insubstantial edifice. "God is now sifting His people, testing their purposes and their motives. Many will be but as chaff—no wheat, no value in them" *(Testimonies,* vol. 4, p. 51).

It is to purify His church that the Lord causes the shaking; and it is to help us seek the full power of the gospel in our lives that the shaking and sifting is of special benefit to us individually (Isa. 6:1-8; Amos 9:9; Matt. 7:21-27). The shaking arouses us from our indolence and complacency. The shaking compels us to know the truth for ourselves, rather than merely to be surrounded by it as with alabaster pillars, cold and sterile, supporting a temple of noble tradition, venerated but unloved. The shaking dislodges from their stately perch those who merely profess the truth, while bearing witness against it by their indifference to Christ and the salvation of others. The shaking exposes the weakness and sterility of every way, every idea, and every sentiment that is false. Whatever is depraved and valueless is brought down forever by the shaking. Thus, the shaking, while it is a most trying experience, is necessary.

The shaking has four principal causes:

1. *Indifference.* A lackluster attitude toward God produces a superficial religious experience. When the cross of Calvary is seen only at a distance, in a faint and foggy light, then the mists of error can easily roll across the landscape of our minds (see Gal. 3:1-3). Nominal believers, who reject the converting influence of truth, become offended and irritated when the truth is brought forth with heightened power and clarity.

"God's Spirit has illuminated every page of Holy Writ, but there are those upon whom it makes little impression. . . . When the shaking comes, by the introduction of false theories, these surface readers, anchored nowhere, are like shifting sand. They slide into any position to suit the tenor of their feelings of bitterness" *(Testimonies to Ministers,* p. 112). Such persons will easily be carried off by a spirit of disaffection and discouragement and by false theories that justify their disgruntled feelings (see 1 John 2:17-21).

But we needn't let the ever-rising tide of apostasy and spurious teaching drive us to despair. "The Lord has allowed matters in our day to come to a crisis, in the exaltation of error above truth, that He, the God of Israel, might work mightily for the greater elevation of His truth in proportion as error is exalted" *(Selected Messages,* book 2, p. 372).

The Lord will arise in vindication of His downtrodden law and violated grace. The true glory of His atonement, its sin-conquering, life-giving power, shall be gloriously revealed (Hab. 3:2-4). And the shaking will clear the way for this.

2. *Heresies.* The Lord always seeks to awaken us to the glory of His ways through the vitalizing power of His Spirit (Rom. 13:11; 1 Cor. 15:34; Eph. 5:14-17), but many doctrinally well-fortified believers slumber on, wrapped in the comforts of this life and the false security of trusting in their knowledge (Matt. 25:1-13; Rev. 3:14-17). Messages of truth, to discerning yet passive listeners, have the welcome sound of a familiar melody that confirms them in the certainty of having the right beliefs (Eze. 33:30-32). No new or repeated declarations of truth awaken in them a love for Christ and humanity. Therefore, as a last reluctant recourse, the Lord permits the church to be shaken by heresies. The introduction of false theories has an agitating effect that compels the church to rise up and earnestly "contend for the faith which was once delivered unto the saints" (Jude 3).

As a result of this process, the truth is brought forth with greater strength, cogency, and appeal than ever before. The more vigorously truth is assaulted, the more valiantly its self-vindicating power is displayed. Some Laodiceans thereby learn to love the truth more and live it out with new commitment and zeal.

"God will arouse His people; if other means fail, heresies will come in among them, which will sift them, separating the chaff from the wheat. The Lord calls upon all who believe His word to awake out of sleep. Precious light has come, appropriate for this time" *(Testimonies,* vol. 5, p. 707).

In this phase of the shaking, the character of those who maintain error in the face of truth is exposed for its weakness and instability. "For there must be also heresies among you, that they which are approved may be made manifest among you" (1 Cor. 11:19). Weymouth translates this verse: "For there must of necessity be differences of opinion among you, in order that it may be plainly seen who are the men of sterling worth among you."

God has given a banner to those who fear Him so that it may be displayed because of His truth (see Ps. 60:4). We are to uphold truth, but not in a divisive, critical spirit. Fanaticism in advocating doctrinal purity is one of the contributing factors in the shaking. False teachings in circulation among us, which cause grievous harm, have provoked some defenders of "pure Adventism" to lash out at the church in a quarrelsome, Jehu-like defense of the faith. This exhibits the wrong spirit. True, the church vitally needs repentance, revival, and reformation. We must openly acknowledge this, but it does not need to be assaulted by self-appointed Elijahs who are far more readily disposed to denounce the church for its sins than to confess their own.

"Of all people in the world, reformers should be the most unselfish, the most kind, the most courteous. In their lives should be seen the true goodness of unselfish deeds. The worker who manifests a lack of courtesy, who shows impatience at the ignorance or waywardness of others, who speaks hastily or acts thoughtlessly, may close the door to hearts so that he can never reach them" *(Gospel Workers,* p. 507).

"We must attend to our own souls diligently. We must walk in humility. We want no war garments on, but the garments of peace and righteousness. May the Lord teach us how to wear His yoke and how to bear His burdens. Everything in this cause and in this work may be accomplished with a kind, conciliating spirit. We may be courteous, always, and never be afraid of being too much so. We must practice showing good will toward all men" *(This Day With God,* p. 83; see also p. 172).

But most of us have met or shall someday meet would-be reformers who persist in being divisive and denunciatory, alleging that the church is too far gone in corruption to be restorable. You may or may not be able to help them, but for your own benefit, you should heed the counsel of Scripture: "Now I urge you, brethren, note those who cause divisions and offenses, contrary to the doctrine which you learned, and avoid them" (Rom. 16:17, NKJV). Contempt for the organized church is a hallmark not of sanctity, but of prideful independence.

O that every Seventh-day Adventist had a copy of Ellen White's *The Remnant Church,* a 63-page compilation on how to relate to God's church and His counsel to it! Those who read and understand this book (available through any Adventist Book Center) could never be led astray into some offshoot movement, no matter how cunningly disguised it may be or how seemingly zealous for the purity of the church.

3. *God's Counsel to Laodicea.* "I asked the meaning of the shaking I had seen, and was shown that it would be caused by the straight testimony called forth by the counsel of the True Witness to the Laodiceans. This will have its effect upon the heart of the receiver, and will lead him to exalt the standard and pour forth the straight truth. Some will not bear this straight testimony. They will rise up against it, and this will cause a shaking among God's people" *(Last Day Events,* p. 175).

But bear in mind that it is those who *reject* the testimony, not those who accept it, who leave the church. Christ's message to Laodicea isn't "Come out" but "Let Me in" (see Rev. 3:20). Faithful respondents to the message let Christ into their hearts, and they stay in the church. The counsel of the True Witness directs us to receive genuine faith that works by love to cleanse the soul, and to obtain Christ's righteousness as a free gift wrought into the heart, and to apply the Word of truth to our own lives through the grace of the Spirit.

This sweeps away all formalistic and pretentious religion. It brings in the everlasting righteousness of Jesus, our Redeemer-King. Those who think they already have this experience, while they really lack it, will be the most keenly offended by Christ's message to Laodicea.

"The shaking of God blows away multitudes like dry leaves" *(Testimonies,* vol. 4, p. 89).

"Chaff like a cloud will be borne away on the wind, even from places where we see only floors of rich wheat" *(ibid.,* vol. 5, p. 180).

"To stand in defense of truth and righteousness when the majority forsake us, to fight the battles of the Lord when champions are few—this will be our test. At this time we must gather warmth from the coldness of others, courage from their cowardice, and loyalty from their treason" *(ibid.,* p. 136).

"The church may appear as about to fall, but it does not fall. It remains, while the sinners in Zion will be sifted out—the chaff separated from the precious wheat. This is a terrible ordeal, but nevertheless it must take place" *(Last Day Events,* p. 180).

We need not make this experience more difficult for ourselves and others by adding to it a spirit of disaffection and disloyalty. We have work enough to repent of our own sins, and come on to higher ground spiritually. Those who do this will have no spare time or inclination to expose the sins of others and castigate the church because of the tares mingled among the wheat. They remember that angels, not angry humans, are to do the work of separation (see Matt. 13:27-30, 40-42).

While it is true that many members will leave the church during the shaking, it is also true that "the ranks will not be diminished" *(Selected Messages,* book 3, p. 422). "The broken ranks will be filled up by those represented by Christ as coming in at the eleventh hour. There are many with whom the Spirit of God is striving. The time of God's destructive judgments is the time of mercy for those who [now] have no opportunity to learn what is truth. Tenderly will the Lord look upon them. His heart of mercy is touched, His hand is still stretched out to save, while the door is closed to those who would not enter. Large numbers will be admitted who in these last days hear the truth for the first time" *(Last Day Events,* p. 182). Under the power of the latter rain, multitudes will leave Babylon and join the remnant church (Rev. 18:1-5; cf. Joel 2:23-32).

4. *Persecution.* Those who welcome the Holy Spirit's presence in their lives shall be willing in the day of God's power to proclaim His truth with uncompromising clarity. Their lives of holy service and morally pure conduct will attest to the authenticity of their message and experience. They will exalt Christ's righteousness. They will herald and humbly exhibit the power of His grace to pardon and sanctify sinners. They will exalt God's law as the standard of character and conduct. They will proclaim the Sabbath as God's end-time seal. They will expose the false position of apostate Christendom as Babylon and warn the world against receiving the mark of the beast, which is compulsory Sunday observance. Those who stand for these unpopular truths will suffer great persecution from the apostate religious world (Matt. 10:16-26; 24:7-9; Gal. 4:29; Rev. 13:11-17).

This indescribably harrowing experience will be of great value in helping purify the remnant church (see Isa. 17:6-8; 24:13-20; 52:1, 2).

"Prosperity multiplies a mass of professors [those who claim to believe]. Adversity purges them out of the church" *(ibid.,* p. 173).

"In this time the gold will be separated from the dross in the church" *(Testimonies,* vol. 5, p. 81).

"In the absence of persecution there have drifted into our ranks men who appear sound and their Christianity unquestionable, but who, if persecution should arise, would go out from us" *(ibid.,* p. 174).

But the persecution inflicted on God's people shall have an unexpected effect outside the present ranks of God's remnant church. "On every occasion that persecution takes place, the witnesses make decisions, either for Christ or against Him. Those who show sympathy for men wrongly condemned, who are not bitter against them, show their attachment for Christ" *(ibid.,* p. 181).

We have briefly glanced at the four major causes for the shaking—indifference, heresies, God's counsel to Laodicea, and persecution. God works through all these factors—including those He does not cause—to effect the unchanging counsels of His will. And all these factors lead up to His second coming. "Yet once, it is a little while, and I will shake the heavens, and the earth, and the sea, and the dry land; and I will shake all nations, *and the desire of all nations shall come"* (Haggai 2:6, 7).

Not only are the world, the nations, and the church shaken, but also every professed believer. Those who truly make the Lord their reliance have a fortitude, a tenacity, a stamina, that is more than human. Laodiceanism, worldliness, heresy, fanaticism, apostasies, persecution, calamities—none of these elements separately or combined can shake God's faithful people out of His church. "For surely I will . . . sift the house of Israel among all nations, as grain is sifted in a sieve; yet not the smallest grain shall fall to the ground" (Amos 9:9, NKJV; cf. Ps. 46:1-5; 125:1, 2; Jude 24, 25). "And it shall come to pass that he who *is left in Zion* and he who *remains in Jerusalem* will be called holy—everyone who is recorded among the living in Jerusalem" (Isa. 4:3, NKJV).

The Lord gives clear instruction on how to stand in the shaking. It's not by might, nor by power, but by His Spirit that people are made spiritually steadfast and invincible. Character determines destiny. "Lord, who may abide in Your tabernacle? Who may dwell in Your holy hill? He who walks uprightly, and works righteousness, and speaks the truth in his heart; he who does not backbite with his tongue, nor does evil to his neighbor, nor does he take up a reproach against his friend. . . . He who does these things shall never be moved" (Ps. 15:1-5, NKJV).

"Those who are true to principle will not be shaken" *(Life Sketches,* p. 93). This is because they are building their lives and characters on the unshakable Rock, Christ Jesus, and His Word (see Luke 6:48). No matter how rigorous the trials or how close the tests, they do not capitulate to Satan's wiliest arts or fiercest pressures. Conscious of their calling and election as God's children, they aspire through the enabling grace of God's Spirit to represent their Saviour aright. Accordingly, they shrink from no service and shun no sacrifice that might bring relief from suffering or salvation from sin. In the time of the shaking their object is not self-preservation, but the redemption of souls and the honor of God.

Many incidents of church history demonstrate the strength and grace of those who remain unshakable. We select here just one inspiring example.

In the 1660s King Charles II of England and his counselors were determined to extinguish clear Bible teaching in their land and bring the people under thinly disguised bondage to Rome. They passed laws making it illegal for any but state-approved ministers to preach in English pulpits. This excluded Baptists, Presbyterians, Puritans, and dissenters of every kind. The penalties for disobedience were fines, whipping, disfigurement, jail, or other indignities as struck the fancy of cruel judges in the king's employ.

John Bunyan, Baptist preacher, came under the force of these edicts of exclusion, and because of his refusal to stop preaching spent many years in jail.

During the early stages of Charles's acts of intolerance, a great plague broke out in London. As the ravages of the plague continued month after month, hundreds died each day. The state-appointed ministers fled their parishes and moved to safer places outside the city. Their vacant pulpits were now left free for the interdicted ministers to preach to the people, who were terrified of the plague and starving for the bread of life. These ministers preached sermons of such power and persuasiveness as the church had not heard for years.

They fearlessly visited the sick in their homes and ministered to them. Under the ministry of these godly preachers, thousands were converted to Christ and His true gospel. They no longer fed on the miserable husks of formalism that their official ministers had dispensed until their cowardly flight from the plague. Thus, through this shaking, God's true servants were made manifest and His gospel was brought forth with distinctness and power.

Finally Christ will arise to shake the earth terribly. This shaking climaxes in a great earthquake that will reduce Babylon to rubble and bring about the collapse of every form of evil on our planet (Isa. 2:10-22; Rev. 16-19). But prior to that time, during the last phase of Christ's intercessory work for rebellious humanity, the shaking has a probationary, redemptive purpose. It exposes the weakness and corruption of the false props on which misguided multitudes lean. Those props come in various forms—dreams, ideas, institutions, and people whose influence is contrary to the gospel and deadly to the soul.

Through the shaking that lays bare the fraudulence and folly of every unscriptural way, the Lord is sending a final message of merciful warning to the world: "Arise and depart, for this is not your rest; because it is defiled, it shall destroy you, even with utter destruction" (Micah 2:10, NKJV). But the warning to arise and depart shows that the door of hope is still open. It is still possible to flee from the wrath to come. As everything that can be shaken is being shaken, to reveal the things that are unshakable, let us examine the nature of our own religious experience. Are there combustible elements in our character? Do we cling to practices and thoughts that war against the work of God's grace in our souls? Is there anything in God's inspired directions that we find distasteful or irritating? If so, it signifies inward trouble. The Lord says: "Do not My words do good to him who walks uprightly?" (verse 7, NKJV).

"The work of apostasy begins in some secret rebellion of the heart against the requirements of God's law. Unholy desires, unlawful ambitions, are cherished and indulged, and unbelief and darkness separate the soul from God. If we do not overcome these evils, they will overcome us" *(Our High Calling,* p. 347).

To wandering Israel the Lord extended this probing counsel: "Who is wise? Let him understand these things. Who is prudent? Let him know them. For the ways of the Lord are right; the righteous walk in them, but transgressors stumble in them" (Hosea 14:9, NKJV). These words are as pertinent today as when Hosea recorded them 2,700 years ago.

> How firm a foundation, ye saints of the Lord,
> Is laid for your faith in His excellent Word!
> What more can He say than to you He hath said,
> To you, who for refuge to Jesus hath fled?
>
> "Fear not, I am with thee, O be not dismayed;
> For I am thy God, and will still give thee aid;
> I'll strengthen thee, help thee, and cause thee to stand,
> Upheld by My righteous, omnipotent hand.
>
> "When through the deep waters I call thee to go,
> The rivers of sorrow shall not overflow;
> For I will be with thee, thy troubles to bless,
> And sanctify to thee thy deepest distress.
>
> "When through fiery trials thy pathway shall lie,
> My grace, all-sufficient, shall be thy supply.
> The flame shall not hurt thee; I only design
> Thy dross to consume, and thy gold to refine.
>
> "The soul that on Jesus hath leaned for repose,
> I will not, I will not desert to his foes;
> That soul, though all hell should endeavor to shake,
> I'll never, no never, no never forsake!"
> —From Rippon's *A Selection of Hymns*

Fair as the Moon, Clear as the Sun

13

A 6,000-year military campaign is drawing to its climactic end. Two hundred generations of humanity have served in this campaign under one of two masters, Christ or Satan. Often the participants have changed sides. The campaign has sometimes been fought with literal weapons, as in the wars between ancient Israel and its heathen foes and some sixteenth-century Reformation churches, which were assailed by European armies loyal to Rome. Generally, however, this prolonged war has been fought not with physical but spiritual armaments. The weapons of the Christian's warfare are not the weapons of the world (see 2 Cor. 10:4, 5); rather they are those of the Spirit employed to demolish Satan's imprisoning strongholds of sin and error.

God's church is His army. Its mission is to bear the tidings of His salvation to a world barricaded in the darkness of superstition and error and amassed in the fortress of unholy living. Following the apostolic era (A.D. 31-100), the church itself had to struggle for centuries to return to the light of truth that became progressively but never completely eclipsed by Satan's fierce efforts to extinguish the torch of its heaven-ignited witness.

In the midst of the church's worst confusion and days of apostasy, there always remained a loyal core of believers, never in the majority, who clung to God's Word as the sole spiritual authority to direct their faith and practice.

Why this mysterious endurance and fortitude among these few breasting unfavorable winds and tide? The answer is found in

119

Jesus' promise: "Upon this rock I will build my church; and the gates of hell shall not prevail against it" (Matt. 16:18). The church is built upon an indestructible foundation, Jesus Christ, and those who build upon the foundation of His truth shall invincibly prevail with it (1 Cor. 3:11; Matt. 7:24, 25).

In the power of Christ, the apostles carried forward the work of evangelizing the world (Acts 4:33; Col. 1:23). Invigorated, instructed, and inspired by the Holy Spirit, they turned multitudes from darkness to the marvelous light of the gospel. People in the remotest parts of earth and the greatest depths of ignorance responded to the energetic, superhuman efforts of God's early witnesses (Zech. 6:12; Acts 12:13-17; 1 Thess. 1:8). But even as God's work progressed through the consecrated efforts of these first-century believers, Satan was drawing into the church treacherous individuals whose chief aim was to exalt and enrich themselves through this vibrant "new" religion (Acts 20:29, 30; Jude 3, 4). Through the seditious work of these spiritual parasites and self-promoters, the way of truth became "evil spoken of" (2 Peter 2:1-3).

The truth is also misrepresented by those who embrace Christianity, or rather a mere semblance of it, out of a desire only to benefit themselves, rather than to honor God and be a blessing to others. Christ dealt with the cases of such in the parable on the wedding garment (Matt. 22:1-14; Isa. 60:10; Rev. 19:7, 8). The person without the "wedding garment" (i.e., Christ's righteousness) wants all the external benefits of the gospel, all the creature comforts of heaven, but desires no character change, no responsibilities in God's service.

But the selfishness and hypocrisy of some do not negate the gospel or the church's message and mission. The existence of religious frauds only attests to the accuracy and needfulness of God's prophetic warnings through Christ and His prophets (Matt. 7:13-15; 24:24; 1 John 2:18, 19).

Truth does not remain obscured forever. Satan is not granted the satisfaction of endlessly keeping all Christendom in partial confusion under the blighting mist of error and corruption. The Lord has decreed that He shall purify unto Himself a peculiar people zealous of good works, a people who shall shine forth fair as the moon, clear as the sun, terrible as an army with banners (Titus 2:12). His zeal shall accomplish this (Isa. 37:31, 32). No devil, no false theology, no collective denial of humanity shall prevail against this Heaven-ordained purpose. Christ shall present to Himself a glorious church, not having spot or wrinkle, or any such thing, but holy and without blemish (Eph. 5:27; cf. Isa. 62:1-5; 2 Cor. 11:2).

God promises that prior to Christ's return all truth and all blessings that Christ has meant to bestow on His church shall be fully restored (Isa. 58:12; Acts 3:21). It is the privilege of every faithful believer to be part of this church. Superior strength, stamina, or spirituality do not secure this privilege. It is gained by simple-hearted (though not simpleminded) reliance on the Lord and His promises. Not by might, nor by power, but by His Spirit the Lord makes His people an invincible force in the world, able to demonstrate the changeless truth and beauty of Heaven's way (Ps. 84:5-7; Zech. 4:6).

"Christ has given to the church a sacred charge. Every member should be a channel through which God can communicate to the world the treasures of His grace, the unsearchable riches of Christ. There is nothing that the Saviour desires so much as agents who will represent to the world His Spirit and His character. There is nothing that the world needs so much as the manifestation through humanity of the Saviour's love. All heaven is waiting for men and women through whom God can reveal the power of Christianity.

"The church is God's agency for the proclamation of truth, empowered by Him to do a special work; and if she is loyal to Him, obedient to all His commandments, there will dwell within her the excellency of divine grace. If she will be true to her allegiance, if she will honor the Lord God of Israel, there is no power that can stand against her" *(The Acts of the Apostles,* p. 600).

Weak, intellectually deficient, ludicrously idealistic, and unfit for the practical requirements of "real" life—this is how the world has generally regarded those who are part of God's church. This attitude predominated in the first-century A.D., as it has in these past three centuries of pseudoenlightenment (1 Cor. 1:18, 25-31; 2:12-15; 2 Cor. 13:4; Rom. 8:35-37; 2 Tim. 4:3, 4). But human philosophies all sink into dusty oblivion, while the truth as it is in Jesus shines forth with increasing luster and unflagging strength from generation to generation (Prov. 4:18; Rev. 14:1-5).

In fact, the indomitable wisdom and power of the gospel is being as dramatically revealed in our time as it was in the apostolic era. Consider, for example, Russia and Eastern Europe. Communism left that part of the world socially, financially, and spiritually bankrupt in less than three generations. The unceremonious collapse of Communism opened the way for the revitalizing influences of the gospel, and in the space of a few years millions have found (and millions more are continuing to find) salvation and soul refreshment that eluded them under the stifling bonds of an ideology that purported to distill the noblest values of the ages. This philosophy even included some of the ethics of Christianity, but had the fatal flaw of denying the Saviour.

In the midst of the present world's upheaval and staggeringly swift changes, the church, instead of exposing itself as impotent, inefficient, and obsolete, has proved to be an instrument of life, grace, hope, and redemptive power. Instead of becoming a fossil of discredited superstition, the church continues to be a fountain of regenerative life, watering the world with grace and hope through its work of practical benevolence: medical care, disaster and famine relief, education—indeed, every kind of humanitarian service and spiritual aid.

More than merely keeping up with the times, the church is ahead of the times, because its vision and agenda are anchored in prophetic certainties and the unfailing relevance of Christ's gospel. Building on a foundation that cannot be shaken or overturned (1 Cor. 3:11; Heb. 12:28), the church is on the march, not a death march or a march of destructive conquest, but a search-and-rescue march to seek and save the lost by the gospel loved, lived, and told. People of goodwill everywhere, like Rahab, welcome the entrance of such an army. Moreover, many join it to aid in its mission and partake of its strength and joys, its sorrows and tribulations, and its ultimate triumph.

But meanwhile, the church is not on a sentimental journey free from hazards or harassment. Rather, in these last days just prior to Christ's return, the church is the target of Satan's concentrated malice and fury (Rev. 12:17). When he cannot corrupt God's people or turn them aside from their mission to carry the gospel to the world, Satan tries to destroy them. But the Lord has a countervailing plan.

"Then the Lord will create over the whole site of Mount Zion and over her assemblies a cloud by day, and smoke and the shining of a flaming fire by night; for over all the glory there will be a canopy and a pavilion. It will be for a shade by day from the heat, and for a refuge and a shelter from the storm and rain" (Isa. 4:5, 6, RSV; cf. Isa. 60:1, 2; John 17:22). He proves to be a mighty protector, an invincible guardian of His flock who follow Him wherever He leads (2 Chron. 16:9; John 10:27-29).

Robert Leighton, seventeenth-century English clergyman, saw to his deep dismay much religious persecution in his time. But he penned these hopeful words: "The church has sometimes been brought to so low and obscure a point, that if you can follow her in history, it is by the track of her blood, and if you would see her, it is by the light of those fires in which her martyrs have been burnt; yet hath she still come through, and survived all that wrath, and still shall till she be made perfectly triumphant!" (in G. S. Bowles, *Illustrative Gatherings,* Second Series, p. 239).

Satan's rage against God's people will intensify as he sees the growing success of their mission to take the full light of the gospel to the world. Working through political and religious leaders who resist the truth, he will stir up a global war, an unprecedented storm of persecution against God's true church (Matt. 24:9; Rev. 13:11-17). This will usher in a time of trouble such as never was since there was a nation. But just then Michael, the Messiah and Prince of Israel, will stand up for His people and rescue them with a spectacular heroism that will dwarf the greatest of human exploits real or imaginary. At that time God's people will be delivered, everyone who will be found written in the book of life of the Lamb slain from the foundation of the world (Dan. 12:1; Rev. 13:8). "And they that be wise shall shine as the brightness of the firmament; and they that turn many to righteousness as the stars for ever and ever" (Dan. 12:3).

"Therefore the redeemed of the Lord shall return, and come with singing unto Zion; and everlasting joy shall be upon their head: they shall obtain gladness and joy; and sorrow and mourning shall flee away" (Isa. 51:11).

"Blessed are those who do His commandments, that they may have the right to the tree of life, and may enter in through the gates into the city" (Rev. 22:14, NKJV).

"These are the ones who have come out of the great tribulation, and have washed their robes and made them white in the blood of the lamb" (Rev. 7:14, NKJV).

"To him who overcomes I will grant to sit with Me on My throne, as I also overcame and sat down with My Father on His throne" (Rev. 3:21, NKJV).

Language is wholly inadequate to portray the supernal glory that awaits God's people in the hour of the church's ultimate triumph and the endless days beyond. "The love of Christ is so broad, so full of glory, that in comparison to it, everything that man esteems so great dwindles into insignificance. When we obtain a view of it, we exclaim, O the depth of the riches of the love that God bestowed upon men in the gift of His only begotten Son!" *(Our High Calling,* p. 366).

The fullness and unchecked flow of this love throughout eternity shall constitute our highest joy in heaven, and all our other joys will result from the inworkings and manifold outflowings of divine love in every being. Best of all, God will be with us, openly, visibly, and wonderfully accessible at all times. His fellowship will surpass all other delights and impart exquisite pleasure to every pursuit, every relationship, every facet of existence. For His is the power, the kingdom, and the glory for ever. Amen!

We should not fail to note one special aspect of the joy God's people will have in heaven. "When the redeemed stand before God, precious souls will respond to their names who are there because of the faithful, patient efforts put forth in their behalf, the entreaties and the earnest persuasions to flee to the Stronghold. Thus those who in this world have been laborers together with God will receive their reward" *(Testimonies,* vol. 8, pp. 196, 197).

"What rejoicing there will be as these redeemed ones meet and greet those who have had a burden in their behalf! And those who have lived, not to please themselves, but to be a blessing to the unfortunate who have had so few blessings—how their hearts will thrill with satisfaction! They will realize the promise, 'Thou shalt be blessed; for they cannot recompense thee: for thou shalt be recompensed at the resurrection of the just'" *(Gospel Workers,* p. 519).

The church has one foundation,
'Tis Jesus Christ her Lord;
She is His new creation,
By water and the word;
From heaven He came and sought her
To be His holy bride;
With His own blood He bought her,
And for her life He died.

Elect from every nation,
Yet one o'er all the earth,
Her charter of salvation,
One Lord, one faith, one birth;
One holy name she blesses,
Partakes one holy food,
And to one hope she presses,
With every grace endued.

Though with a scornful wonder,
Men see her sore oppressed,
Though foes would rend asunder
The Rock where she doth rest,
Yet saints their faith are keeping,
Their cry goes up, "How long?"
And soon the night of weeping
Shall be the morn of song.

'Mid toil and tribulation,
And tumult of her war,
She waits the consummation
Of peace forevermore;
Till with the vision glorious
Her longing eyes are blest,
And the great church victorious
Shall be the church at rest.

—Samuel J. Stone

The crowning delight of that glorious rest shall be the Father's song of welcome, which He, as a full sharer of the nuptial delight, shall sing upon receiving Christ's royal bride into the heavenly kingdom. "The Lord thy God . . . will rejoice over thee with joy; he will rest in his love, he will joy over thee with singing" (Zeph. 3:17).

"And I heard as it were the voice of a great multitude, and as the voice of many waters, and as the voice of mighty thunderings, saying, Alleluia: for the Lord God omnipotent reigneth. Let us be glad and rejoice, and give honour to him: for the marriage of the Lamb is come, and his wife hath made herself ready. And to her was granted that she should be arrayed in fine linen, clean and white: for the fine linen is the righteousness of saints. And he saith unto me, Write, Blessed are they which are called unto the marriage supper of the Lamb" (Rev. 19:6-9).

That day is not far off now when those words shall resound in heaven amid all the glorified throng of the redeemed. Why not resolve by God's grace to be a subject of His jubilant hymn of welcome and join in singing the Song of Moses, the servant of God, and the Song of the Lamb, to the eternal honor and glory of Him who has ransomed His royal bride with His own blood?

Zephaniah 3:17

Welcome home, ransomed souls of Mine!
Welcome to this place of peace,
Where nevermore your hearts shall pine
For heaven's balm or pain's surcease.
Your bliss is bought with My Son's blood,
Forever ending sin's dark flood.
Evermore with Me you'll dwell,
Evermore in realms of light
Where joys extend and praises swell
With rapturous wonder and pure delight,
For by My gospel all is well.
Yea, forever, all is well.

Epilogue

"Christ designs that heaven's order, heaven's plan of government, heaven's divine harmony, shall be represented in His church on earth. Thus in His people He is glorified. Through them the Sun of Righteousness will shine with undimmed luster to the world. Christ has given to His church ample facilities, that He may receive a large revenue of glory from His redeemed, purchased possession. He has bestowed upon His people capabilities and blessings that they may represent His own sufficiency. The church, endowed with the righteousness of Christ, is His depositary, in which the riches of His mercy, His grace, and His love are to appear in full and final display. Christ looks upon His people in their purity and perfection, as the reward of His humiliation, and the supplement of His glory—Christ, the great Center, from whom radiates all glory" *(The Desire of Ages,* p. 680).